VOICES OF OUR MOUNTAIN KIN

VOICES OF OUR MOUNTAIN KIN
Folklore and Traditions from the Southern
Appalachian Mountains

Edited by
Jerry Owen, Linda Anders and
Pamela Yarborough

Cover and book layout design by
Robert T. Yarborough

Andborough Publishing • Colorado

First Andborough Publishing edition

Copyright© The MountainKin Group 2006

First Edition 2006

All rights reserved.
No part of this publication may be reproduced or transmitted in any form or by any means, electronic or mechanical, including photocopying, recording, or any information storage and retrieval system or technologies now known or later developed invented, without permission in writing from the publisher.

Publishers Cataloging-in-Publication Data

Owen, Jerry, Anders, Linda, and Yarborough, Pamela, eds.
   Voices of our mountain kin: folklore and traditions from the southern appalachian mountains/compiled and edited by Jerry Owen, Linda Anders, and Pamela Yarborough; introduction by Jerry Owen and Linda Anders.
      p.cm
   Includes index
   ISBN - 13 978-0-9774181-2-1
   ISBN - 10 0-9774181-2-X
   1. History. 2. Folklore. 3. Genealogy.
   I. Owen, Jerry, cp. II. Title.
Library of Congress Control Number: 2006929349

Cover and book layout design by Robert T. Yarborough

Printed in the United States of America

Andborough Publishing, LLC.
4935 Sprangler Drive
Colorado Springs, Colorado 80922

*Dedicated
with love and thanks
to our mountian ancestors*

Contents

Introduction	xi

Chapter One: Ghosts, Superstitions and Beliefs — 15

Mountain Ghostbuster	17
Catheryne Faison Hufham Wynne	19
The Little People	22
Uncle Avery	25
Paranormal and My Ancestors	26
The Poisoned Apples	27
The Clock of Life and Death	28
Hainted Hollow	29
The Hen Crows	30
Cherokee Heritage, the Burning Bush	31
Cherokee Hollow	33
Links with the Past	35
One Last Match	37
My Life's Record	40
The Altar	41

Chapter Two: Civil War in the Mountains — 45

Andrew Jackson Owen	47
Camp Douglas Letter	48
Civil War Experiences	50
Jim Wilson's Prank	52
Nellie Dunn Sizemore's Tragic Life	52
Hendersons at War	54
Civil War Deserters	56
Alfred Owen Hides in the Haystack	57
Civil War Story	59
Mountain Faith After the Civil War	60
A Father's Love for his Son	61
Marauders	63
The Experiences of a Soldier's Wife	64

Chapter Three: Moonshinin' & Cookin' — 77

- Revenuers — 79
- Saved From the Revenuers — 84
- Sunday Dinner - Sweet Potato and Possum Pie — 86
- Mountain Food Stories — 87
- Possum Hunting — 88
- Grandmother Mary Lee — 88
- The Beans Burned — 89
- Buttermilk Trail — 90
- Moonshinin' — 91
- Childhood Memories — 91
- July Supper — 92

Chapter Four: Healin', Dowsin' and Cauls — 95

- Healing, Dowsing and Cauls — 97
- Mountain Healing — 97
- Wart Healing — 98
- Wart Curing — 99
- Mountain Medicine — 99
- Cauls — 100
- Dowsing — 100

Chapter Five: Mountain People and Their History — 103

- Lynch's Law — 105
- Mountain Prank — 106
- Little Ruf's Trick — 107
- Pearson and Amanda Queen Owen — 108
- A Mountain Love Story — 110
- Leaving the Mountains — 116
- A Visit to Wolf Mountain — 119
- The Cherry Tree Incident — 122
- Memories of a Granny — 123
- Metal Monster — 128
- Ollie's Sewing Machine — 129
- Boney's Defeat — 129
- Saree Crack — 130
- Memories of my Nanny — 132
- Life Story of Perry Fields Gravley — 134

Chapter Six: Owen Hymn   142

Photographs and Illustrations:

John Asbury Owen Family	18
Catheryne Wynne	19
Mary "Polly" Norris Rhodes	31
Vance, Akin, Albert, Mattie, Ivy and Allice Owen	38
Bessie Lee Gravely Anders	42
Andrew Jackson Owen	47
Camp Douglas Letter	49
Civil War Reunion	50
Thomas Wilburn Rhodes	60
Mountain in Towns County, Georgia	80
Arthur Tillman "Slim" Owen	107
Pearson & Amanda Queen Owen	109
Little Owen Schoolhouse	115
Julia Owen & Lylish Eller	117
Thomas Rhodes and Family	119
Florence & Rufus Owen with daughter Grace	125
Sarah E Rhodes Owen	131
Perry Fields Gravley	135

Index   145

INTRODUCTION

The stories in this book are dedicated to the ancestors of our group, MountainKin. MountainKin is an email group of family history and genealogy researchers who descend from mountain folks. We were originally created in 2001 with three main goals. Our first goal was to trace and record the lives and histories of our ancestors who lived and died in the foothills and mountains of the Blue Ridge, Balsam and Great Smoky Mountains. Our second goal was to bring as many of their descendants together in yearly reunions in the heart of our beautiful mountains as we possibly could. Our third goal was to work together to protect and preserve the mountains and the mountain heritage of our ancestors. We have worked diligently since that time to accomplish those goals.

The book you are about to enjoy is another group effort in protecting and preserving our mountain heritage and, by extension, the mountains themselves. Many of our beloved mountains have fallen victim to commercialism and venture capitalists. We realize that the old ways of mountain life are quickly disappearing in the same way as has the Native American way of life. This book of mountain tales will help preserve a small portion of this fading way of life.

Early in the 1700's, many of our ancestors first encountered the beautiful mountains and valleys that our group calls home. This land which we love and honor so much was at that time inhabited by the great and proud Cherokee. According to an old family tradition, an agreement was struck between some of the pioneers and the Cherokee. According to this agreement, the settlers would be allowed to live in the valleys for as long as they were willing to live by the law of the Cherokee and to faithfully do everything within their power to keep out other unwanted white settlers. This relationship proved to be a good one and this group of pioneers never suffered the terrible fate of many early settlers. They remained friends with the Cherokee right down to the time of the Cherokee Removal in 1838. In fact, many of the pioneers intermarried with the Cherokee and took on many native traditions and beliefs, which can be found in the descendants of these families today. Other traditions were passed down through the generations from the "old country", including the Elizabethan way of speech and the closeness of the family clan. The beautiful, lush mountains even reminded them of the hills of Scotland, Wales and Ireland.

Many of the old family names still live on in this fertile valley even today. All one has to do is drive up through the tall mountains, down through the valley, and along the banks of the life-giving French Broad river to spot mailboxes with the names Owen, Galloway, Reid, Glazener, Hoxit or Hogsed, Whitmire, Parker, Patterson, McCall and Gillespie. Other descendants of these same and other pioneer families, now scattered all across our great nation, have reunited with our cousins who still live in this blessed land and formed a group known as MountainKin. The group has lovingly assumed the responsibility of helping to protect and preserve the mountain way of life, extending that defense also to the great Cherokee and all that we have inherited from their traditions.

It is in honor of both our ancestors and their neighbors, the Cherokee, that we dedicate this small book of mountain tales. It is our grand privilege to be able to save and share as many tales from the mountains as we possibly can. In this endeavor we look forward to continuing to gather many more ancestral tales for inclusion in future books such as this.

We sincerely hope that these tales of mountain life will bring as much pleasure to you as they have brought us.

          Jerry Owen, MountainKin Founder
                  and
          Linda Owen Anders, MountainKin Co-coordinator

Voices of Our Mountain Kin

CHAPTER I
GHOSTS, SUPERSTITIONS AND BELIEFS

"Superstitions are, for the most part, but the shadows of great truths."
-Tryon Edwards, 1809 - 1894
American Theologian

Mountain Ghostbuster
by Jerry Owen

One of my ancestral relatives was an original ghostbuster in the mountains of Northeast Georgia. My Grandfather Owen used to love to talk about him all the time. His name was John Owen (of course it was), and he was a man who had no fear. Anytime he would hear about a "haint" anywhere in the mountains, he would take a couple of friends and set off to prove or disprove it.

On one such occasion he heard about this old mountain cemetery that was supposed to be haunted by a ghost in flowing white robes each night at 12 midnight. So he and his two friends rode their horses for a couple of hours until they reached the place. They arrived right around midnight, and as soon as they got there, they saw the ghostly figure. Sure enough it was wailing and it appeared to be shimmering white in the glow of the moon which created quite an eerie feeling. As soon as the apparition began to cry and wail, his two friends spurred their horses and took off down the trail for home, leaving him alone with the ghost.

Even though he was a little shook up, he got down off his horse and slowly walked toward the wailing specter. As soon as he got close enough, he saw that it was not a ghost at all but a young woman from a nearby mountain home. It turned out that her young child had died of a fever about a year before, and in her grief, she would get up every night, walk to the graveyard and cry over her baby. John took her on his horse and gave her a ride back home. That pretty well ended that ghost story.

He was always eager to find out the truth behind any and all ghost stories. Sometimes they did not turn out like this one though. On another such ghost busting trip, he and his friends went to this old mountain church which was supposed to be haunted by a red-eyed demon. Again the story was that around midnight (these ghosts must have a thing about midnight), this creature would come out from behind the pulpit of the church and would actually attack anyone foolish enough to be around at that time. So they went inside and sat on the back row of the old church and waited in the dark until midnight. They were laughing and joking about it when midnight came, and then suddenly they heard a noise.

Looking towards the front of the building, they saw what appeared to be two glowing red eyes slowly moving in their direction. Just as John was telling his friends to stand their ground, they both jumped up and ran to their horses. I think maybe he should have picked braver ghostbusting buddies.

(John Asbury Owens Family) Left to Right: Edith, Leathy Stiles, baby Robert, Elba, John Asbury, Johnny, and James Lawrence

John decided he would just wait and see what it was. The closer it got to him, the more he sensed something really bad about this apparition. He would later tell everyone that even though he feared nothing, he felt that only a fool would not know when the real "running time was here". John jumped up when the eyes were within about 5 feet of him, ran out the door, jumped on his horse and took off down the trail. Just as he did, something jumped on behind him and wrapped its arms around him, cackling and laughing hysterically in a high pitched voice that John said he would never forget as long as he lived. He just kept riding and eventually whatever it was let go and was gone.

John Owen didn't let this one little incident stop his ghostbusting and continued to hunt for haints in those mountains until he was a very old man. So you see I think it's in my DNA to explore cemeteries.

Catheryne Faison Hufham Wynne

by Catherine Gage Wedge

Catheryne Faison Hufham Wynne

My grandmother, Catheryne Faison Hufham Wynne, was actually born in Hickory, NC, in 1898, but her mother, Robbie Gage Hufham, was born in Marshall, NC, and grew up in the mountains. The family lore was that of the mountains, and my grandmother often related events in her life that to others may have seemed fantastic, but which she believed she had actually experienced. She had a very sad life, so this may have made her more prone to the spiritual side of things, and to "seeing through the veil" as it were.

Catheryne was raised from the age of 11 by her grandmother, Mary.

The women in the family by that time had no men kin around to support them, so while Robbie, Catheryne's mother, was off earning her living, Catheryne and her Grandmother Mary, and Catherine Yancey Hawkins, the great-grandmother, all carried on and tried to make ends meet by running a boarding house. My grandmother had to carry wood and fetch water and often was left to "dump the slops" after the boarding house guests departed. One evening she was sent to a nearby spring to draw water to wash up the kitchen. It was about twilight and the walk to the spring was through woods reported to be haunted by the Cherokee who had been so cruelly sent from the land generations before. (Unbeknownst to my grandmother, it so happens that she herself was probably part Cherokee--a fact I have uncovered these many years since.)

When she came to the spring, suddenly a great, towering figure loomed over her. She swore until the day she died that it was an Indian chieftain in full war regalia. The figure stood over her with its arms crossed, saying nothing. Being a child, and unwilling to hang around and see what the figure wanted, my grandmother dropped her bucket and took to her heels, never stopping until she had run all the way home down the hill from the spring and was safe inside with the kitchen door slammed tight and locked behind her. She was punished for failing in her task, but she didn't care. She never would go back to that spring after dark for all the rest of the years she remained in the mountains no matter what consequences were set for her. (Knowing what I now know, I have to wonder if the visitor wasn't trying to make some kind of contact with my unsuspecting grandmother, but never had the chance due her flight.)

Catheryne's Grandmother Mary died instantly in 1911 of a stroke or an aneurism. Catheryne was 13. She wed young, being 16 at the time of her marriage. No doubt she married to escape the drudgery of her life as a quasi-servant. My grandfather played ball with the minor leagues, and the team traveled throughout the state for matches and exhibition games. One day the team passed through the town where my grandmother was living and put up at her great-grandmother's boarding house.

My grandfather stood six feet tall, with blazing blue eyes; he had handsome athlete's physique in his youth. He was thirty-one when he met my grandmother there. She was a tiny girl, four foot eleven in her stocking feet, with coal black hair and deep green eyes. He saw this young woman who was so heavily burdened with hard work and, feeling sorry for her, began to draw her out about her life. She told the story of how they sat in the front porch swing one hot summer evening when she had some free time, and the gentleman reached in his pocket and pulled out the first silver dollar she had ever seen. He handed it to her, telling her it was hers to keep. She said she would never after forget the kind gift of this great, handsome stranger who very soon became her husband. She rarely referred to him by his first name, which was William. For all the years I can remember, she would call out to him: "Mr. Wynne, what do you want for your supper?", and he in turn would reply: "Catheryne, I don't care so long as it's hot and on a clean plate." Or: "Mr. Wynne I'm going uptown now, " she'd say, and he would reply something muffled from behind the sports section of the paper.

Their first-born son, William Jr., was the spitting image of his father. When he was nine years old, a sturdier, more robust specimen of boyhood had never been seen in their town. Billy, as he was called, was also a born entrepreneur, selling lemonade, planning businesses, arranging sales, and he was obviously destined to start his own company one day. His doting parents could not have been more proud. That year, when my mother was two, her big brother Billy was bitten by a rabid puppy and died. The child had the shots (they existed even in the 1920's) but not in time, and the first-born son of the family died an agonizing and lingering death.

My grandmother maintained that she often saw Billy around the house after his death, at odd moments for many, many years afterwards. She would come into a room, she said, and there he would be, large as life, smiling at her. Then he would simply vanish into thin air. Billy never spoke, and she said his presence was never, ever frightening. She thought he had come to give her reassurance and comfort, and so it was, until one day he never came back again. Perhaps she no longer had need for his visits.

Other things "haunted her" throughout her life. Strange footsteps on the roof with no one up there, things appearing and disappearing without cause, and the like, happened to her frequently, and she passed this sixth sense down through the generations along the female line even so far as to me and on through my daughter.

The Little People
by Jerry Owen

James Owen died in 1892, leaving a last will and testament which we have found in the Towns County, Georgia Courthouse. As a result of this will, my great-grandfather, William Sherman Owen, a grandson of James, received land on a beautiful mountain which straddles the Georgia, North Carolina border. This mountain sits half in Clay County, NC and half in Towns County, GA. Here in this picturesque setting William Sherman and Sarah Elizabeth Rhodes Owen reared a family of 10 children. My grandfather Jesse Luon Owen was number seven.

My grandfather was only eight years old when the Owen family left these mountains and came to Texas, but he never lost his love and longing for his mountain home. As a child he listened hungrily to every story told and retained these memories perfectly, passing them on to his children and grandchildren. For this I am eternally grateful and hope to be able to save his mountain stories for many generations to come. His mountain stories passed on to him by his parents involve many different aspects of life in the mountains, including everything from daily chores and mountain haints to Civil War stories. These stories stretch back in time to when James Owen lived in what is now Transylvania County, NC as well as to the time the family lived in Towns County, GA. My grandfather was an example of the old adage "You can take the boy from the mountains, but you can't take the mountains from the boy". The following is one of those simple but real family stories.

Jesse's mother, Sarah Elizabeth Rhodes Owen, was a very strict disciplinarian and constantly instilled Christian values and hard work ethics into her children. Sarah followed the hard-shell fundamentalist Baptist religious faith and expected her children to do the same. Missing church on Sunday was not an option and neither was any sort of slacking at chores. The punishment for infractions of these rules was swift and severe. The place where these punishments were carried out was the family smokehouse. Every family had a smokehouse where meat was smoked and cured as well as other items stored. If one of the boys or girls failed to live up to Sarah's high standards, they would be formally escorted to the smokehouse where a cat-o-nine tails and an extra razor strap was kept. Either one of these instruments of education were very unpleasant. My grandfather said that, being one of the younger children, he did not experience quite the severe discipline of the elder children, but what he did receive from these two carryovers from the Inquisition left an indelible impression on him and he believed they made a better man out of him.

Even though Sarah was extremely religious, she also allowed Native American beliefs to intermingle with her solid Christian teachings. The reason for this was that her grandmother, Mary "Polly" Norris Rhodes, was a full-blooded Cherokee who avoided the Cherokee removal by hiding in the mountains. Just as you cannot take the mountains from the boy, you cannot remove all traces and vestiges of Cherokee belief from the Christian. This combination makes for a very powerful and strong personality, and this is what Sarah truly was, a very powerful woman, who later became the matriarch of the Owen family.

On one particular occasion the three older boys, Selly, Paul and Marson Owen, were working in the family garden down on the side of the mountain in a small cove clearing. The entire family had been working the garden earlier in the day but Sherman, Sarah and the other children had returned home to take care of chores and prepare supper while these three remained in the garden working until the sun began to set. Paul Owen was around 14 or 15 years old at the time and he corroborated this story in 1997.

One of the Cherokee beliefs the boys had learned was that there are a race of little people who live in and around mountain coves and peaks and occasionally allow themselves to be seen by the big folks. The belief was that as long as you were friendly to them and did not bring harm to their way of life then they were friendly to you. However if you were unfriendly then you had best watch yourself. Calamities might befall you such as your house or barn burning, livestock dying, or worse. The Owen boys could not help but have some thoughts that these might actually exist. In fact they had always been very careful to show their respect to any possible little folks by leaving small portions of any food they had under tree stumps just as their grandmother had taught them. On this night they especially became strong believers in these little people.

As they were working down the garden rows side by side, Paul said, they began to hear strange little noises that sounded like singing but far away. Knowing that no one was around, they just chalked it up to being tired. It just so happened that a storm was brewing in the mountains and, from the looks of the clouds and the sounds of the thunder, they decided it best to get back to the house. Just about that time the small voices became very distinct, and it seemed that there was a great multitude of voices all around them. They became very excited and took off running back towards home. After they were about half way back up the hill towards the home cabin, they saw a flash of lightening and heard a crash behind them. When they looked back, they saw that the lightening had crashed right where they were working the garden.

Years later they all agreed that it was possible that the little people had warned them or it was possible that their strong intuition had given them all three warnings at the same time. Either way, their lives were spared that day. They were very excited when they returned home and shared this joy and excitement with the family.

You might think they would have slept peacefully that night but, as we all know, there is sometimes another side to the story and this one became very evident to the boys as they lay down that night. Almost simultaneously they realized they had made a terrible mistake. One of the very strict rules Sarah enforced was the care and safety of farm implements. Selly, Paul, and Marson, in all the excitement, had left the hoes they were using behind in the garden. They knew that they could not leave the house in the middle of the night without being detected because Sarah and Sherman were light sleepers and the large mountain dogs would surely betray them. It was not uncommon for Sherman to shoot his shotgun into the darkness when the dogs began howling, and the boys definitely didn't want any part of that. The only thing they could do was just take whatever punishment came their way when the family retrieved the hoes for the next day's work. This was a very serious infraction because these hoes were a vital part of the family food supply. Being left out overnight was a big no-no, because of the dampness of the mountain.

Just after sunrise the next morning, after the family breakfast and chores, everyone walked to the shed to retrieve their equipment. All three boys would later say that those last few steps were some of the longest they ever took. It was all they could do to not blurt out apologies before the crime was even discovered. They could already begin to feel the heat from the strapping they knew was coming their way. Unbelievably, when Sherman opened the door to the shed, there were all three of their hoes sitting with the rest of the family's farm implements. The boys never said a word to anyone for years about this part of the story and it was only after Sarah had passed away in 1962 that they dared tell this. As far as their own speculation as to what happened, they all three believed it very possible that the little people had saved their lives with the lightening and saved their behinds from a strapping by returning the hoes to the shed in the middle of the night. From then on they were especially careful to show respect to the old Cherokee beliefs, even though they remained faithful to their mother's Baptist upbringing. They continued to leave food under the trees as long as they lived in those mountains.

Uncle Avery
by Saoirse

My Uncle Avery was walking along the dirt road on the hill in back of his house in 1946 when he heard a wagon coming. He stepped out of the road to let it pass. It passed. He felt the breeze from it and could even smell the sweat of the horses, but it just wasn't there--he saw nothing.

Less than 2 weeks later, he was dead. He fell off the back of a wagon while carving a prancing colt and stabbed himself in the heart with his own pocket knife.

Paranormal and My Ancestors
by Gordon Owen

Regarding paranormal, I've inherited it from both sides. My maternal grandmother's parents had dinner at 4 PM. She was 12 or 13 when she interrupted the dinner table conversation to calmly state "Uncle Thurston just died" before her eyes rolled back in her head and she slid off her chair. It took weeks for word to get from Cedro Wooly, Washington, to Franklin, North Carolina, that Thurston's fatal logging accident took place a few minutes after 1 PM Pacific time.

In her elder years, that good woman's prayers included a fervent appeal on behalf of her descendants. My mother told me the exact words: "Lead them, guide them, and protect them unto the third and fourth generation." Sometimes it was "Lead them, Lord. Guide them and protect them in everything they think and say and do."

I taught my wife's friend Melodie (Irish-Norwegian) how to dowse. She learned almost instantly and was delighted. Proving the point that any good thing can be perverted, she went home and began asking questions of the dowsing rods, telling them to close for yes and open for no. Just like a (expletive deleted) Ouija board. Whatever she connected with answered enough questions to identify itself as an English lady who had died in the 1800s and was going to be Melodie's spirit guide.

When she came over the following evening, she wanted to demonstrate and had her dowsing rods ready to go. I was uncomfortable and wary as she asked the rods "Is there anyone here who was there?" The rods snapped together. "Is there anyone here you'd like to talk with?" Instead of opening or closing for yes/no, both rods immediately swiveled to point straight at me. I felt the "fight or flight" surge of adrenaline as I was overwhelmed by a sense of something ancient, evil, and intensely male. When I opened my mouth to say "I won't talk to it," what came out was "I won't talk to it, but you can ask it whether it was a male when it lived on this planet before the time of Enoch." Melodie reported that the rods went dead in her hands as I spoke.

A strange enough experience and I'm sure different people will have various explanations for the words that came to me. I can't explain them, but maybe I was led. And guided, and protected.

The Poisoned Apples
by Mary Ellen Yelton

Ollie Hoyle was my grandmother. A more humble, caring, sweet person I have never met. She lived in Balsam with her husband, Gill and their children. It seems that Gill had a bad habit of leaving home and roaming for weeks at a time. His family never knew where he was or when he would be back. One dark, rainy night while he was gone on one of his "trips", a feeble knock came at the front door of their house in Balsam, N.C. Ollie answered the door. There stood an old hag of a woman, dressed in black, long stringy gray hair, carrying a big burlap sack. She asked to come in to get warm as she was soaking wet. Ollie, at first, would not agree and the woman begged. Being such a compassionate person, she agreed, reluctantly.

The old woman warmed herself and knew it was time to move on. She reached way down in her burlap sack and gave each child a shiny red apple. What a treat!! Being poor, the family was excited and could almost taste the juicy apples. After the old woman left, my grandmother grabbed the apples from her children and threw them in the fire!! While the children cried and begged for the apples, Ollie told them she was afraid the old woman, a stranger, was a witch and had poisoned the apples!!

I guess the mountain folk had heard of and were leery of anyone who might have been a witch!

The Clock of Life and Death
by Jerry Owen

In our Owen family are several stories and artifacts that are quite authentic. This story involves an old clock which has been in the family for at least 150 years and maybe longer. The clock was the pride and joy of my 2nd great grandfather, William Jackson Owen.

Sometime in 1889 William Jackson "Jackie" lost his temper and kicked an old cow that refused to move from the pasture to the barn. According to my Grandfather Jesse Owen, Jackie had quite a bad temper and this time it cost him dearly, or maybe we could say his karma caught up with him, because the cow kicked back and put him in the bed with some pretty severe injuries. He might have recovered from the cow kick but pneumonia set in and back then that was an extremely dangerous thing.

My great-grandmother, Sarah Elizabeth Rhodes Owen, Jackie's daughter-in-law, sat with him several days. Eventually he lost the fight and died while she was sitting with him. Before he died he told Sarah he wanted her to have his clock. The clock was in the room where he was in bed and, according to Sarah, this clock which had never stopped running suddenly stopped at the exact hour, minute, and second he crossed over.

Sarah kept the clock but for the longest time no one could get it to run again until one day a stranger passed through the mountains. He traded fixing the clock for a good hot meal of baked possum and sweet potato pie. From that day forward the clock worked perfectly until Sarah died on January 26, 1962 in Dallas, Texas. On that day her daughter, Oner Owen Ward, was sitting up with her and Oner testified that on the exact hour, minute and second she crossed over the clock stopped and to my knowledge has never been started up again. One interesting side note is that Sarah was one fourth Cherokee.

Hainted Hollow
by Kathy Owens

Don and I once lived in "hainted hollow". We built our home new there, but something was definitely wrong. The front door was kept locked, but at night it would come open on its own. We finally put on dead bolts and it stopped.

Our family tried to tell us that it was a new house and it was "settling" and that's what made the door come open. Well, we heard something fall one night. It sounded like the huge bookcases in our living room had fallen; it actually shook the floors. There was nothing there.

Then we started having a "visitor". One night a "little" man came and stood at the foot of our bed. It woke Don and me both up, I could feel him stand over me, and Don actually saw him, barely visible at the foot of the bed. We were both paralyzed with fear for a few seconds, and the little man ran from the room and down the hall. We could hear him. Don jumped up, turned on the light and couldn't find a thing. It was cold winter time and both of our sons were snuggled deep in their covers, actually snoring. It couldn't have been one of them.

We never felt him in our room again, but often strange things would happen in our household. The silverware (of course ours wasn't ever real silver) and our soup bowls and glasses would "disappear"; then they would come back after being gone for weeks. Strange? I'll say. I finally named him "George". Whenever anything was missing or something strange happened, one of us would say "George is at it again".

Sometimes I would be in front of the mirror brushing my hair and George would dash behind me, his quick reflection in the mirror. You know how you get the impression that something ran behind you. It was unnerving, but we finally decided that whatever it was, it wasn't going to hurt us.

However, it was so bad, that most of the time we kept silent about it, for fear that our families would think that we were mentally ill.

Then we bought an old "mom and pop" grocery store, out in the country. This old store had high ceilings and the original wooden floors. Guess who came to work with us? George!! We had one particular box of Jello that would fly off of the shelf. I'm not kidding. I picked that box up so many times, I grew tired of it. I'm telling you, we ALL saw that box fly. I finally wedged it between other boxes of Jello to keep it on the shelf.

Okay, so I've admitted that my family is a little "strange". Don and I moved after the children were grown. We've not heard from George since.

Ghosts or real? We don't know what George was; we just know that your imagination DOES NOT wake both of you up.

THE HEN CROWS
by April Montgomery

William Hudgens was a mean man. Many called him wicked. Life was hard in the late nineteenth century and, like many farmers of Western North Carolina, William was bad to drink, and drinking only made things worse.

It was February 1890 and William was crossing a foot log over a creek near his house when a hen leapt onto his chest. He was unable to knock the hen away and then she did a very strange, but not unheard of, thing--the hen crowed. She crowed three times before leaping away to go about her own business.

William believed that God had, in those moments, chosen to reveal Himself, and William knew that his death was not far off. He knew he would die in 3 hours, 3 days, 3 weeks, 3 months or 3 years. This revelation was enough to change William's life. He accepted Christ. He is remembered for his prayers, not only for himself and his family, but for the future generations of his family.

William died 3 years later to the day of the hen incident, February 18, 1893.

Cherokee Heritage, the Burning Bush

by Jerry Owen

I would like to share another story that has been in our family for many generations. My 3rd great-grandmother, Mary "Polly" Norris, was born in 1826 high in the mountains of Macon County, North Carolina. According to family oral history, she was a full-blooded Cherokee. As you will see, that has been difficult to verify because of what happened in this story. In 1844 Polly married my 3rd great-grandfather, Milton Rhodes in Haywood County, North Carolina, where the Rhodes family lived.

In 1838 most of her friends and many of her family were escorted to Oklahoma on what has come to be called the Trail of Tears. In fact another of my 3rd great-grandfathers, James Owen, was a member of the North Carolina militia that helped escort the Cherokees on this sad journey. There were several Cherokees who hid out in the mountains rather than take this insane exile to a place where even the white man did not want to live.

Mary was one of the brave Cherokee women who refused to go. I know she was in some way connected to a Cherokee resistance group that included the great Cherokee martyr Tsali. Later one of her grandsons, my great uncle, would assume the name Selly which was a safer way of using the name in the white world.

Through the efforts of a great man by the name of Thomas, a place was later set aside for the remaining Cherokee in NC.

Mary "Polly" Norris Rhodes (standing)

Along with this land, each of the Cherokee would be paid a certain amount of money if they would just come in and register. Many of the Cherokee signed and took the money. Some, however, did not trust the government at all but saw it as a trap and continued to remain in hiding. Mary was one of the non-trusters. Several of her family urged her to go in and take the money. She did consider this for a short time, but a most unusual thing happened to her that changed her mind.

One day she was going up a mountain trail picking blackberries and other wild berries to make pies. After she had gotten about half way up the mountain, she saw what looked like smoke just off the trail and behind a large rock. Being curious she walked off the trail and made her way to the rock. Years later, she would say that the sight she beheld behind that rock froze the blood in her veins. Just beyond this large rock formation was a bush approximately four feet tall. What terrified her was that the bush was totally engulfed in flames. It was a strange-colored flame, more blue than anything else. As she stood there speechless, it occurred to her that the bush was not burning up to cinders but just continuing to burn. She approached just close enough to see if it was really fire, and she said it was so hot it singed all the hair off her eyebrows. This was verified later by other family members. Just as she started to turn and run suddenly a voice spoke to her from the burning bush (no we didn't steal this story from Moses).

The bush spoke to her for a few minutes and then, she later said, she passed out and fell on the ground. She was missing all that day and night. Sometime the next day she came straggling in with all her clothes tattered and her hair singed, talking complete gibberish. After she regained her senses and told the story, everyone who believed her, and even some who didn't, wanted to know what the bush told her. To her dying day she would never utter a word of it. But she never ever took the money from the government.

GHOSTS, SUPERSTITIONS AND BELIEFS

CHEROKEE HOLLOW
by Sam Owen and the Ol' Man

Aaron Styles was a proud young man. Proud of his English heritage, his good looks, straight black hair and strong Christian up-bringing. In truth, he had little else. Leading a sway-backed mule with his pregnant bride and their meager possessions aboard, Aaron headed west, in search of a new and hopefully better life. His Paw had not taken kindly to his taking a half-breed for his wife. Maybe people in this county would not be so hateful. Settin' his sights on that bald face of what would later be called Grandfather Mountain, Aaron pondered what would lay ahead for his new family in this place called "Transylvania".

In search of a sweet spring for their new homestead, Aaron followed a likely stream upward and up still farther into a hollow shaded by stout chestnut trees. There, in the upper reaches of the hollow, was the spring and the clearing where he built a home for his bride. Their first winter in the mostly finished cabin proved bitter cold. Aaron found time from his chores to construct a cradle for what, he hoped, would be his first son. With the spring thaw, came the time for the birth of their child. A scream from his wife brought Aaron running inside from his morning wash. As night fell, she still struggled to rid herself of the burden within her. Sometime after midnight, Aaron's son was born, still and quiet, no life in his little body. Dawn broke, but the sun never reached the cold, fog-choked hollow.

After a sleepless night spent holding his sobbing wife, Aaron set about digging a small grave for his unnamed son. As he dug, his mind wandered. He thought how difficult it was going to be to scratch out a little garden in this flinty soil. When he reached what he thought to be the proper depth for burying such a small body, Aaron realized he had uncovered a small arrowhead. He picked it out and rubbed it with his thumb. It had been crafted of white quartz. Strange, he thought, that it had been so deep. Although arrowheads were numerous in this area, most were found at or near the surface. He dropped it back in the grave, thinking maybe it somehow belonged there.

Back then, the closest preacher was a twelve mile ride down the mountain. So, Aaron and his wife stood alone at their son's grave. He took off his old hat, looked to the clouds and asked out loud for God to look kindly on their little one, as He must have had some reason for taking him.

The next winter brought a new pregnancy and the spring brought another still-born child, this one a little girl. Aaron made another grave next to his son's and, yes, in the bottom was a white arrowhead. Cold fear shook Aaron's body. He vowed to God at that time not to make any more babies with his wife.

The years passed. The couple never spoke of their children and no more did they try to conceive. Aaron tried to drown his sorrow in home brew, while his once lovely wife drowned hers in pone and gravy.

The Ol' Man said that was the end of the story. But I knew better. Over the years, I had picked up pieces here and there. I knew our family owned about eight acres up in Cherokee Hollow. I did not know why none of us were allowed to build up there. Maybe a childhood memory of "Indian haunts" told by a cousin over in Lake Toxaway. (At the time, I didn't much believe her cuz she was a "teenager", but she was real purty and I did have a small crush on her.)

Last night, when the Ol' Man had near kilt hisself on corn likker, I talked the rest of the story out of him. Turns out Aaron's wife had died in her sleep one night in the late fall. The next day, even the thought of digging another grave on that ground sent chills up his spine. After much contemplation and more than a few trips to the spring house, where he kept his jug, Aaron had reached a decision. Using much of his split fire wood, he built a pyre in their little cabin for his wife's funeral. When the house and his wife had turned to embers, Aaron Styles turned and walked westward, but his tortured soul remained in Cherokee Hollow.

Links with the Past
by Jerry Owen

I have had or know of some strange experiences connected to cemeteries. During a visit to the mountains, Winnie and Steve Kropelnicki were giving me a tour of old homesteads and cemeteries. One of the places they took me was to the burial site of James William and Lucretia Dillard Reid, my 4th great-grandparents. They are buried on the side of Hogback Mountain in Transylvania County, NC, but you have to know which little road to drive up to find them.

A few years before, Winnie was trying to find these graves, but she did not have a clue as to which road to take. They were her 2nd great-grandparents so she was really anxious to find them. She said she was just driving along beside Hogback when all of a sudden a feeling came over her to turn off on the next little winding dirt path. She said it was really a strong urge so she turned even though she was a little worried about her car and the ruts. She said she hadn't driven very far until another urge came over her to stop the car and get out and look around through the growth. Immediately she found the graves, covered in weeds and grass. These stones have since been replaced with new ones and the surrounding area is much better kept, but she says she just knew that something led her to those graves. I think they wanted to be found.

Another similar story happened back in 2001 to my brother and me. We were on a kick to find as many of our North Carolina and Georgia families who had migrated to Oklahoma as possible. Some of the family names we were searching for were Parker, Brown, Owen, Glazener, and Burch. It seems that sometime around the turn of the century there were several families who made this move. One in particular I was interested in finding was Prince Pulaski Edward Glazener. Prince Pulaski was the son of William Jasper and Margaret Caroline Owen Glazener. Margaret Caroline was a daughter of James Owen and Lizzie Parker. She was also a sister to my 2nd great-grandfather, William Jackson Owen. Margaret Caroline and William Jasper were married just in time for him to go off to fight in the War Between the States, but not before the act of procreation apparently, because little Prince Pulaski Glazener was born in 1862. His dad never returned from the war. Margaret Caroline later married James Wylie Walker and had several children with him. Prince Pulaski was left to live with his grandparents, James and Elizabeth, where he grew to manhood. When James died he left Prince Pulaski a little money to start his life.

I always felt a connection with the love between James and his grandson and was strongly motivated to find out as much as I could about Prince Pulaski and his final resting place. It turned out he wasn't all that far away from me. When Prince Pulaski moved to Oklahoma, he settled in Love County. Love County is only about 50 miles from where I live just across the Red River from Cooke County TX. My brother and I drove up there several times and eventually even met his living daughter-in-law who was in her late 90's.

The cemetery story happened on our first visit to Marietta in Love County, OK. We had discovered he was buried in a cemetery close to town, so we looked at several that day. Remember this was before all these cemeteries started going online, so we were doing it the old-fashioned way, with my brother starting on one end and me the other and just walking the whole cemetery.

Finally the sun was beginning to set and we'd had no luck, and even began to think maybe Price Pulaski did not have a marker and our entire effort was for nothing. We asked several people for directions to any out of the way places and followed them, all to no avail. It was beginning to get dark. You know, that time just before the sun goes down and the rays are very pretty but getting dimmer by the second. We had a long way to go so we decided to head home. Just as we were driving out of Marietta, something struck me that we should turn down this little road and follow it. My brother thought I was just wasting time, but I followed the little road until it led us just outside of town. Wouldn't you know it, there was a cemetery and the very first rather large marker read "P P Glazener." Talk about being excited. I was excited and I felt inside myself that something special had just happened there in that place. I still feel that way. I think it was something to do with real love never dying, and the ties we create here on earth being forever.

The Mountain Firebox: One Last Match
By Jerry Owen and Fredna Laura Owen Meredeith

This story takes place in the vast primitive range of mountains that connect Southwest North Carolina with Northeast Georgia. In the 1860's James and Elizabeth Owen sold their mountain property in North Carolina to James's brother-in-law, Jehu McCall, and bought a large section of mountain land in Towns County, Georgia from James's uncle by marriage, Isaac Glazener. This became the new home for all of James and Elizabeth Owen's family for many years to come. It was a far less populated and more uncivilized country and that suited James just fine.

James passed away in 1892, leaving Elizabeth the matriarch of the family. Elizabeth was from very old sturdy mountain stock, being the daughter of William Solomon Parker, Sr. She was a strong matriarch for the family, and all Owen family business worked its way through her.

Occasionally there would be a need to pass along family news and other information between Georgia and North Carolina. Elizabeth "Lizzie" would always use one of her sons or grandsons for this as opposed to the mail carriers who weren't all that reliable or fast back in those days. This story involves one of those times. Important family news needed to be passed along, and she chose two of her grandchildren for the job. It would have been quite an arduous task in good weather, but this particular news needed to be delivered in the middle of winter. Snow was quite high in the mountains and it was extremely cold. The two Owen boys chosen for the harrowing task were Pulaski Akin Owen and Thomas Vannete Owen, approximately 19 and 14 years old. Everyone in the family just called them Akin and Vance.

Akin and Vance set off on the trip with all the excitement common to young boys of that age. They made good time under the circumstances on the way to Transylvania County, NC and, to their good fortune, the weather held out fairly well. After having a good visit back with all the relatives, they loaded up their knapsacks with lots of provisions and letters from relatives and headed back towards home. Unfortunately their luck did not hold out on the return trip, and they were caught in a terrible snow blizzard. It was one of the worst storms in years and they were slowed down considerably just trying to not freeze to death. Snow storms also brought out a lot of hungry predators, and they had to take turns standing guard anytime they stopped to rest. The only places to rest in a storm were caves in the sides of mountains. Much of their travel was done through the dark Nantahala forest, and at night they heard all sorts of wild animals screaming and crashing through the dense woods. These two were brave boys, but as the storm worsened, they began to fear they might never see home again.

Vance, Akin, Albert, Mattie (Ledford), Ivy, and Allice Owen

Ghosts, Superstitions and Beliefs

In those mountains many previous generations of travelers, including Cherokee Indians, had left behind a system of what could be called, for lack of a better word, "fireboxes." These fireboxes were sometimes just crude pits surrounded by rocks and some were more sophisticated in design, but the purpose was to give travelers a place to build a fire. I suppose it could be likened to the rest stops along the highways today, but much less evolved. Akin and Vance were just about to freeze to death, shivering and soaked to the bone, when they happened upon one of these fireboxes. They immediately felt a surge of renewed hope and gathered up as much wood as possible. Much of this wood was very wet and they knew it was going to be very hard to start a fire. They used as much dry material as they could for kindling, including some of the packed material in their knapsacks. They had a small box of matches which held only about 10 matches. These were long crude matches and not nearly as efficient as today's butane lighters. They blocked off the wind and began to use the matches to light the fire, but due to the fact that some of the matches themselves had become damp and the constant wind blowing, they did not have very good luck starting the fire. In just a short time they were down to the very last match.

Both Akin and Vance knew this was a defining moment for their future lives. Like all other young folks, they had never taken their religion very seriously even though their mother and grandmother was constantly trying to force it into their heads and hearts. Both mother and grandmother, Owen and Parker, were fundamentalist hard-shell Baptist in belief. Now, Akin and Vance both looked at one another and realized that this one match was all that stood between them and eternity. If this last match did not light the fire, they would surely freeze to death during the night. Almost in unison, they both closed their eyes and uttered a heartfelt prayer to God asking for His help and promising Him that, if they ever got home alive, they would live their lives as a testimony to Him. Amazingly when they struck the last match, the fire began immediately. They said they both looked to the heavens and said "thank you, thank you, thank you". After Akin and Vance made it home safely they were true to their word and both lived exemplary lives, both raising several fine respectful sons and daughters of their own.

My Life's Record
by Bessie Lee Gravley Anders

When my life is over,
what will my record show?
Will it show enough faith,
that he will really know?
I accept his invitation,
to his kingdom up above,
will it show enough of works?
Or show enough of love?

I don't take the time to look
and see what he will see.
Will he say, come in my child
and have a sip with me?
Or will he say, depart from me
your name's not in my book?
Then I'll know, it is too late
to stop and have a look.
Oh Lord! Have mercy on me,
while I'm still on this earth,
that I shall take the time to see
just what my life is worth.
So when my record's open
you'll be pleased with what you see
and then you'll say, "Come in my child
and have a sip with me."

As I look around me at the world as it is today
and see so many people
just throwing their lives away.
If only they'd put their attention
on things from up above,
we would take the hate that's in their hearts
and refill it with his love.

So when their record's opened
he would be pleased with what he sees
and then he'd say, "Come in my child
and have a sip with me."

The Altar
by Bessie Lee Gravley Anders

It was around the family altar
Where I learned to pray.
I remember mamma,
you could always hear her say,
"God thank you for my children,
they mean so much to me.
May they accept salvation
and return the praise to thee."

Now I have grown older
and have children of my own.
If it wasn't for the altar
I may have never known
this glorious, sweet salvation
brought on by a mother's care.
All because she mentioned
us by name in prayer.

I still use an altar
and when I kneel to pray,
I remember mamma
and you can always hear me say,
"God, I thank you for my children,
they mean so much to me.
May they accept salvation
and return the praise to thee."

Bessie Lee Gravley Anders

Ghosts, Superstitions and Beliefs

VOICES OF OUR MOUNTAIN KIN

Chapter 2
Civil War in the Mountains

"If future generations are to remember us with gratitude rather than contempt, we must leave them more than the miracles of technology. We must leave them a glimpse of the world as it was in the beginning, not just after we got through with it."
            -Lyndon B. Johnson 1908-1973
            Thirty-seventh American President

ANDREW JACKSON OWEN
by James Grant

Andrew Jackson Owen came home (whether awol or not isn't known) from the war around Christmas time of 1864 because his wife, MaryAnn, was very pregnant with my great-grandfather, James Milford. After James' birth in January of 1865, Jackson decided to stay at home and take care of his family because James' birth had been a particularly difficult one for MaryAnn.

One day in late February, the Owen homestead was paid a visit by a band of Union troops (the commander wasn't named) who summarily gave Jackson the "option" of either being taken prisoner as a Confederate deserter, or "volunteering" for the Union Army. He was told that if he refused to "volunteer" he would surely be shot, his home burned, and his farm destroyed. Needless to say, with a "choice" such as that, he readily agreed to become a member of the Union Army.

Andrew Jackson Owen

Then after being a Union soldier for only a couple of months, the war ended (April, 1865) and Jackson returned home to his family to live. He died an old man at Wolf Mountain, Jackson County, NC and is buried there, surrounded by his family.

Camp Douglas Letter

transcribed by Katie Gillespie

Camp Douglas, Illinois
Feb.15th 1864

Dear Companion,

With pleasure I seate myself down in order to inform you at this time and hoping these lines reach you in due time, and find you all well, and doing well. I have nothing sharing to write to you.

I want you to do the best you can for yourself and don't be uneasy about me, for I fair very well here now, I get plenty to eat here. I want to see you and the children the worst I ever did in my life, and I want you to write me as soon as you can, and let me know how you are all getting along?, there in that Country which would be a great pleasure to me to hear. WL Boren is here and are well also. BW Burin is here and is well, and Asa Paterson and sons are well.

I can't write much news now so I will close for the present hoping to hear from you soon.

I remain your Companion until death.

(Malinda C. Chappel & A. J. Chappel)

Envelope reads:
A.J. Chappel
Prisioner of War
Camp Douglas, ILL.
Camp K. 62 Regt
NC Troops

Mrs M.C. Chappel
Eastatohee, Pickens District
South Carolina

Via City Point, Flag of Truce

This is a true copy of a letter written to AJ Chappel's wife from him during the Civil War or War Between the States

*Camp Douglas Letter from A.J Chappel to Mrs M.C. Chappel
15 February 1864*

CIVIL WAR EXPERIENCES
transcribed by Linda Anders

This is a letter written by Benjamin James "Jim" Wilson, (b. 2 Jan 1840 – d. 10 Feb 1922), about his experiences during the War Between the States. He enlisted 15 June 1861, in Transylvania County, NC, Company E, 25th NC Infantry, was paroled at Appomattox 9 Apr 1865; M. W. Ransom's Brigade. Jim was the son of Benjamin and Jane Grant Wilson.

After his return from the war, he married Phoebe Serena Bracken on 5 Oct 1865 in Transylvania County. They are my great-great-grandparents and are both buried at Cathey's Creek Baptist Church Cemetery.

Spelling is as written in Benjamin James Wilson's own hand. Unfortunately, the original letter was lost.

Reception for Civil War Veterans, 14 August 1911 at Transylvania Co, NC
Benjamin James Wilson second row, fifth from the right, standing in front of the flag.
Original print located in Mary Jane McCrary Collection,
Transylvania County Library, Brevard, NC

During the War of States I volunteered in 61 in Co. E 25 NC. Our first fight was in front of Richmon Va. 7 days fight ending at Malvern Hill. Next was at Plimoth NC where we flanked them captured 250 prisners. Then went back to Va. Was in nerley all of the fights in Va at Sarps Burg Marland we had to fall back across the Potomack River. At fredricks Burg they tride to break our lines 7 colums deep. We refuted them with heavy loss to them. Our loss was small.

In front of Peters Burg Va they blode up our works. Rushed in the grves to hold works had Black flag. We was frmed out in open field to charge them out. We killed them out. I was wonded in right lung. Ball broke rib lodged between rib and skin. Dr. Lucky was Dr. of our regiment. He sayd I woud not live 15 min. Would not cut ball out. Dr. ohagen came along cut ball out. Then they put me in ambulance cart. I remember when I com to I saw coffin by my bunk. I sayd to ward master hoo is ded he told me had it there to put me in didn't have time to bery me that day. I told him I was not redy for it yet. The Dr. there rote to capton graves of our co that I was ded. He rote it home to Mother that I was dead.

After I got well anuff went back and was in severl fights after that was with Gen. Lee at the surrender. So I will close by saying give my love and respects to all the Daughters of the Cofedarcy.

B J Wilson

When I went to the war we had 4 hed of horses 10 hed of cattle 45 hed hogs 50 hed of sheep. Wen I came back robers had taken all. The first election after the war som of the outliers tride to kill me & would if hadent bin too big coward.

Letter penned by Benjamin James Wilson about his experiences during the Civil War

Jim Wilson's Prank
by Linda Anders

Benjamin James "Jim" Wilson was famous for his sense of humor. I suppose he had seen so much suffering during the Civil War that he just couldn't be serious about the "little things".

My mother tells a story of how he went to visit a neighbor and was invited to stay for lunch. The neighbor's wife was about to send a child down to the spring house on the creek to get some milk to go with the meal when Jim told her there was no need to do that. He said he had just come by there and the spring house had been washed away during the storm the night before. Everything in it was gone. The lady of the house was, of course, very distressed because that was where she kept her milk, buttermilk, and butter. They went ahead and ate lunch and had a fine meal without the milk although they all lamented over the loss.

The neighbor said he would walk part way home with Jim so he could check out the damage to the spring house. When they came to the creek, there was the spring house, completely intact with no damage at all! Jim bent over double laughing about the joke he had played!

Nellie Dunn Sizemore's Tragic Life
by Linda Anders

As I was growing up my grandmother often told me of her grandmother, Nellie Dunn Sizemore. Nellie was only 4 feet 10 inches tall, of Dutch ancestry, my grandmother said. But it wasn't until I was grown and after my grandmother died that I learned the truly tragic story from my great-aunt, Florence Galloway McKinney.

Nellie was disowned by her family when she married John Sizemore in the 1860's. My Aunt Florence never told me why Nellie's family did not like John, but I have found in my research that he may have been part Indian. While that is something that many people would like to claim now, it was not acceptable at that time.

When John left to join the Confederate army, Nellie struggled to survive on her own. Also, she was pregnant with their first child. Unexpectedly, the baby came very early and was not one baby, but twins. Nellie was alone and had to deliver them herself and cut the cords. The babies did not make it. Still alone, Nellie dug graves and buried them.

One of her brothers, also serving in the Confederate army, heard what had happened to his sister. He left his unit and returned home to check on her. He had just ridden into her yard when a group of men caught up with him and shot him as a deserter. They left him there to die. Nellie had hidden from the soldiers and when she came out, she found her brother. She dragged his body into her house and prepared him for burial.

Nellie's husband John was able to come home for a little while near the end of the war but then left and never returned home after the war. He was presumed dead. Nellie had a little reminder of him, however--her little girl, Hattie. With Hattie, Nellie was not able to continue living alone, so she took a job as a servant in the home of a Bryson family. She hoped her life had taken a turn for the better, but one night Mr. Bryson broke into her room and raped her. Nine months later she had another little girl, Mary Jane. Mary Jane went by the last name of Sizemore, Nellie's married name, but everyone knew she was not a child of John Sizemore. Now Nellie was an outcast from society. She struggled for another ten years to raise her two daughters by herself. Finally, in 1880, she married again.

I don't know much about her life with her second husband, but I hope it was more peaceful and that she enjoyed some happiness.

HENDERSONS AT WAR

by Ray M. Henderson. Submitted by Rene` Henderson

Amanda Garner Henderson, the wife of my great-great-grandfather and William M. Henderson's older brother, Nathaniel Howard Henderson, was a woman who had dreams. She once had a dream that no mother should have. She dreamed that four of her sons had gone away to war and never came back home. Early in the war, William Carson Henderson, their oldest son, died at Johns Island, SC, after being shot in the neck while serving in the Confederate Army. James died in a Union prison camp in 1862. George Columbus, who was also in the Confederate Army, died later from yellow fever in Richmond, Virginia.

These three young men and their brother, Lafayette, had left home and joined the Confederate Army without telling their parents they were leaving. Perhaps the reason for their sneaking off to the war was because Nathaniel Howard Henderson, their father, was probably an anti-slavery Unionist like his brother, Lorenzo Dow.

The story of their fourth son, Lafayette Henderson, was, indeed, a tragic tale. "Fate," as he was called, joined the Confederate Army at about the age of seventeen. He was a company musician who served in the 69th NC Cavalry. Fate was captured by Union forces late in the war but somehow managed to escape and make his way back to his mountain home in Cathey's Creek, Transylvania County, NC. He had used a "Yankee" uniform during his escape, and that was what he was wearing when he reached home.

Upon returning, one of the first things that Fate wanted to do was attend his church. Times were so bad that there was nothing for him to wear except the Union uniform. Friends and family warned him that it was not a good idea to wear it in public, but Fate, being stubborn, like many Hendersons, went to church in the uniform anyway. His uniform stirred up quite a lot of talk against him and friends told him that he had enemies and should be more careful because it was dangerous times. Fate also showed up at a dance to play his fiddle, which again caused much talk. Friends, once again, warned him to get rid of the uniform and stay out of sight.

It seems that Fate had other problems as well. While he was away in the war, his young wife, Ruth, had begun seeing a man named Hendrix, a deserter from the 69th NC. Hendrix spread rumors that Fate was a "Yankee" spy, even though, of course, a spy would never wear a Union uniform.

By this time Union forces occupied much of the North Carolina Mountains. When word reached them of an escaped Confederate prisoner, they sent soldiers to Fate's house to capture him. It seems reasonable to believe that the man who reported Fate's whereabouts was probably Hendrix.

Fate was not at home, but the Union men vigorously questioned his father, Nathaniel Howard Henderson. When Nathaniel Howard would not tell them where Fate was hiding, the Union soldiers arrested him and took him to jail.

Later, Union soldiers returned to look for Fate and found only his mother at home. Amanda was afraid and refused to let them in the house. They tried to break in but she had barricaded the door. One Union man managed to get his arm through the door and fired his pistol several times. The intruder quickly removed his arm after Amanda grabbed an ax and chopped at his arm. The Union men left the premises and took their wounded comrade with them. They also took all of the Henderson's horses and mules and never returned

With her husband in jail and Fate hiding in the mountains, Amanda Garner Henderson was left on her own with seven children. She knew where Fate was hiding and would regularly carry food to him. In the meantime, Hendrix was not only turning opinion against Fate, but he was also openly seeing Fate's wife. When this news reached Fate, he decided that he was going to have to kill Hendrix.

Fate found Hendrix and his father working on their farm in the spring of 1865. While hiding behind a stump in the woods, Fate fired his musket at Hendrix. Unfortunately, Fate was apparently a better musician than a marksman. He missed Hendrix and killed Hendrix's father instead. Fate returned to his mountain hideaway while Hendrix and his friends began looking for him.

One day when Amanda went out to take Fate some more food, she could not find him. She returned every day and frantically looked for him. Finally, she found his bullet-riddled body. Hendrix and his friends had apparently found him first. With her bare hands, she dug his grave and covered it with stones.

After her fourth son's death, Amanda lost her mind. Though she looked many times, she could never find Fate's grave again. Afterwards, even after the war, whenever she would hear riders approaching, she would bundle up the silverware and hide it from the "Yankees".

The tragic tale of Fate Henderson did not end with his murder or the war. In 1870, five years after Fate's death, his fourteen-year-old younger brother, Lorenzo Dow, disappeared from his home in the middle of the night. His parents, Nathaniel Howard and Amanda, later discovered that he had left with some neighbors on a wagon train bound for Texas. The night before leaving for Texas, Lorenzo Dow Henderson had avenged his brother's death, by killing Hendrix. He would not return to the North Carolina Mountains until he was an old man; he never saw his parents again.

CIVIL WAR DESERTERS
by Tammy Beavers

My 2nd great-grandfather kept deserting from the Civil War to come back, check on the family and get in the crops. He almost got caught one time when they were looking for deserters. His wife sat on his shoulders with her hoop dress and acted like she was churning butter. She told the men looking that she hadn't seen him but she wished he would come home.

I believe most of the men who deserted just wanted to take care of their families.

Alfred Owen Hides in a Haystack
by Winnie Owen Kropelnicki

John B. Owen was a happy family man when the Civil War began. He lived on a mountain farm with his loving wife Malinda and small but growing family. John's farm was in an idyllic valley situated between several majestic mountain peaks. This area was known as the Gloucester Valley and was rich with wildlife and fertile ground. The Owen family felt safe and secure from the problems of the outside world. They worked hard in the fields during the day and enjoyed the fruits of their labor each evening. Malinda was an exceptional mountain woman who not only prepared meals fit for kings but served all of her neighbors as a midwife and mountain doctor.

John Owen did not have slaves and had no interest in entering this war which was now raging between the North and the South. The beautiful Gloucester Valley is situated in Southwestern North Carolina not all that far from Tennessee. Therefore, it was not uncommon for stragglers from both sides of the war to occasionally pass through the valley. John Owen held the same old-time values of hospitality that had run in his family for as long as anyone could remember. Anyone who found themselves near his home in the evening would be welcome to partake of a fine meal prepared by Malinda and stay with the family until the sun was high over the hills the following morning.

It was this same sense of hospitality which eventually brought trouble to the Owen family. John Owen opened his home to any and all strangers regardless of the color of their skin or their uniforms. Because of this some of his neighbors began to see him as being disloyal to the Confederacy and therefore disloyal to North Carolina. This was a charge which could easily bring death to a man in those times.

One day the authorities of the local area decided to deliver John an ultimatum and force him to make a choice. Soon a large group of men were riding toward the Owen home. This group included not only the local authorities but also the dreaded home guard that many times looked forward to just such situations to bring down their own version of justice on otherwise peaceful folks. On this day John and his two sons, Alfred Henry and Tillman Owen, were working in the hayfield situated above their home. They could easily see the long line of men on horseback slowly winding their way down the switchback which was the only way through the mountains. At this time Alfred was 16 years old, and John feared that they would force his son to join the Confederate army. John loved his family and could not bear the thought of losing any of them to this unholy war. John told Alfred to crawl inside one of the tall haystacks that dotted his field. He told him to remain there regardless of what was said or done and not to come out until someone came for him. Alfred did as his father told him, so that when the group finally arrived at the field, there were only two people there, John and his younger son, Tillman.

The leader of the group knew John personally and had a high respect for him, but proceeded to read him a list of charges. On this list were several occasions wherein John was accused of "harboring Yankees". John defended himself by informing them of the many times he had fed and sheltered Rebels as well. This was of little consolation to the men and, after conferring together, the leader told John that he had one of two choices. He could either join them and ride back to town with his horse and pistols where he would join the Confederate cause, or he could face the justice of the Home Guard which would have meant death for him. John was anything but a fool so he told them that he would be happy to return with them and join the cause. He did tell them that first he would like to have them all join the family for supper and personally experience his hospitality. This was agreeable to them and it was said later that Malinda's cooking actually raised John's esteem in the eyes of these men.

For Alfred, this was a most agonizing time. From his place in the haystack he could hear everything that was said in the field. Alfred loved his father and wanted more than anything to come out and stand by his side, or to offer himself instead of his dad, but he was also a very obedient son and could not bear to go against his father's orders. He would say later that, as the night grew darker and he could smell the aroma of the food from making its way up the mountain slope, he thought he was going to starve to death in that haystack. It wasn't until much later that Tillman was able to slip out and bring a plate of food to him. This was the same food he always ate, but on this night, it tasted better than he could ever remember.

John kept his word and joined the Confederate army. Since he owned his own horse and pistols, he was immediately commissioned as a Lieutenant. John served the Confederacy throughout the war with great distinction and valor, being wounded on more than one occasion. Just before the war was over, Alfred slipped across the mountains to Tennessee where he joined the Yankee army. Fortunately he joined right at the end of the war and never actually had to engage in any fighting, so father and son never had to shoot at one another.

CIVIL WAR STORY
by Saoirse

Daddy used to tell me how Grandpa John took Grandma Myra with him to war. When he got to camp, he found out he couldn't get rations for her. So in December, he got permission to take her to her Daddy's home on the NC/GA line. It is told how they had been traveling, were really tired and the river was frozen. So they made a lean-to, covered it with branches so it would look like something just caught up in the freeze. When they woke the next morning, they found out there had been a deep snow during the night that totally covered their lean-to. They spent another day or two on the frozen river.

One official report states that Grandpa John said he couldn't get back to his lines because Thomas' Legion had the roads cut off.

The copy I have of his pension application says that he was wounded, went to a field hospital and a doctor told him to go home. He was rejected because there was no record of him seeing a doctor. They also said a doctor would not have had the authority to send him home.

He fought for his pension and finally won it just shortly before he died. But he was charged with the cost of a horse and an army carbine he had when he took Grandma Myra home.

MOUNTAIN FAITH AFTER THE CIVIL WAR
by Catherine Gage Wedge

This short anecdote speaks to the devotion and deep religious commitment our ancestors had to their faith and also demonstrates the sly humor they possessed under even the most difficult of conditions. The Major Gage referred to is my 2nd great-grandfather, Robert Samuel Gage, born in 1833 in Hendersonville, NC. He served as a Major in the CSA for three and a half years during the Civil War, having enlisted as a private in 1861. Robert was a "cripple" (his words) having been afflicted with "white swelling", or TB of the bone, since young adulthood. His Confederate rank as a Major was no doubt due to his previous training as a lawyer and a schoolteacher and his ability to keep excellent written records. Robert was not a fighting man. He was in charge of the Commissary for Clingman's Brigade and served under Roswell Ripley.

However, Robert was commended for bravery and diligence to duty under fire during the week-long shelling of Fort Moultrie Sullivan's Island in South Carolina. (This episode of the War has been commemorated in the movie; "Glory".)

At the time of this incident, the War was over and the entire South was struggling to survive and rebuild during a time of great deprivation and scarcity. Robert had settled in Marshall, NC, where he had spent his young manhood.

The River Hill Baptist Church in Marshall, NC, was not active for a period of time during the war. Afterward, a house of worship was built on Blannahassett Island with about fifty members. The first pastor of the church in the new building was Rev. Henry Gilbert who lived at Big Indian Creek, a distance of about twenty miles from Marshall. Brother Gilbert had to walk this distance to pastor the church.

At the time of one appointed meeting, the earth was covered with snow and ice. There was some doubt about Brother Gilbert's coming. Some church members were watching for his appearing, and finally, in the far distance, they could discern an object. As the object drew nearer, they found it to be Brother Gilbert wrapped from head to toe in an old shawl. Major Gage, a strong supporter of the Baptist cause and owner of a dry goods store near where the court house now stands, was one of the observers. After the meeting, Major Gage gave Brother Gilbert a nice overcoat. Brother Gilbert told Major Gage he didn't know when he could pay for the overcoat. Major said, "Brother Gilbert, I do not charge you anything, only to leave the shawl at home."

Major Gage and his wife, Mary Siddall Hawkins Gage, remained lifelong residents of Marshall and devout Baptists.

Based on an excerpt from the history of the River Hill Baptist Church, in Marshall, NC.

A Father's Love for His Son
by Jerry Owen

In 1861 Thomas Wilburn Rhodes was a 16 year old boy living on a farm in Macon County, North Carolina. He felt it was his duty to join the army and fight the Yankee invaders, so he asked his mother and father for permission to do so. Of course his parents were absolutely against this and told him in no uncertain terms NO!!

Thomas's dad, Milton Rhodes, thought the world of his boy and was not about to lose him to some Yankee bullet. Many of Thomas's young friends were excited by the possibilities of becoming local heroes in the eyes of the young ladies. They conspired amongst themselves to slip out of their homes, meet at a chosen location one night, and all run away to the army together. Thomas was very determined to join them. On the chosen night, he slipped out of the house at midnight when everyone was asleep and made his way to the rendezvous. These young boys made their way to the Confederate encampment and promptly became soldiers. Those who already owned weapons were made Corporals. Thomas owned a brace of colt pistols and so immediately enlisted as Corporal T.W. Rhodes.

When Milton and Mary could not find Thomas the next day, they realized what had happened and both were devastated. Mary became depressed, and Milton was extremely angry at first. He soon realized that the only possible course for him was to go, find his son, and either get him back or stay with him in the hopes of protecting him.

Upon finding Thomas, he soon determined that the army had no intentions of releasing his boy. At first he was allowed to stay as a civilian courier and errand runner but later was admitted into the army himself. In this way Milton felt he could at least be around for his son if he was needed. Thomas soon became very sick, and Milton was allowed to take him home to either die or be healed by his mother. After Thomas was much better, he returned to his post with the army but due to his absence was reduced in ranks to a private. This happened in 1863.

Thomas Wilburn Rhodes

Thomas and his father participated in several battles including Petersburg. They were there at the time the Yankees blew the big hole known as the Crater in an effort to undermine the Confederate line. Milton was wounded at the battle of Atlanta and eventually made his way home.

Thomas found himself with a group that was defending Spanish Fort and Mobile, Alabama at the end of the war. At Spanish Fort, he volunteered to stay behind with a small group in order to allow the bulk of the Confederate army to slip away during the night. Thomas, along with around one hundred brave volunteers, put up such a fight that the Union forces were thoroughly deceived and did not realize they had been duped until the next morning. He and what remained of this small band of heroes were captured and imprisoned at Ship Island and eventually moved to Vicksburg, Mississippi where he was released as soon as the war concluded.

Marauders

by April Montgomery

Richard Whiteside built a beautiful home in Cooper's Gap, North Carolina in 1859. Everything, even the windows, was handmade. The timber was cut from his own property to build this home for his family. He was 51 years old and married with 8 children. Total cost to build the house, $563.

The Civil War came soon after the completion of his house and his family was not untouched by it. Marauders or draft dodgers hid in the hills above Cooper's Gap and would often come down to steal food and horses or anything of value from the hard working farming families below. On one occasion, the news came that the marauders were about and up to no good.

So Richard and his family went to work. They had to hide anything that could be stolen; food, animals, anything and everything. This time, they had hidden their meat in the walls of the house.

The marauders came, demanding to know where things had been hidden. The family refused to tell. Thinking an incentive might make the family more forthcoming with the information, one of the marauders brought hot coals into the hallway. Richard stood ready with a bucket of water to douse the flames should they spread, knowing the marauders would most likely gun him down if he moved.

One of Richard's daughters, becoming increasingly hysterical and fearing that they really intended to burn the house down and most likely the family with it, told the men where the family had hidden the meat

The marauders proceeded to tear out the wall and take the meat. They did not burn the house down but did leave a scorched spot on the hall floor as a reminder.

The house still stands today... nearly 150 years after its completion and resided in by Richard's great grandson.

The Experiences of a Soldier's Wife

by Mrs. Robert Franklin (Mary Middleton) Orr
submitted by Dennis Smith

This is a true story of my gg-grandmother (Narcissus (Beck) Middleton), ten of her children and one grandchild. It was written by Mary, her second oldest daughter.

Robert Franklin Orr and I were married in January, 1862. In the fall of the same year he was taken to the Confederate army, and stayed there until, in the spring of 1863, he ran away and came home. He said he would not go back to the Confederate army, and stayed at home until in the fall, when they made up a company of about seventy-five or 100 men and went to the "Yankees" as we then called them. I begged him not to go in the army any more; but he told me not to say a word to him, for he had been driven from his home and he intended to fight his way back, which he did.

So I was left alone. My father (Kinston Middleton) also went with Robert F. to the Yankees; and my mother was left too, with nine children and I with one child; that made twelve of us in all. My mother was poor and times were hard and she could not keep me. My father-in-law (Robert Orr), who lived in Transylvania County, heard that I was alone and sent a wagon for me and moved me to his house.

I went to my father-in-law in March 1864 and stayed there until the middle of August, when, as my sister-in-law and I were out milking, we saw a crowd coming. We were frightened; it was something uncommon to see a crowd unless it was soldiers, for people were afraid to travel, times were getting too close. But when they came up, we saw it was my mother and the children. It was about sixteen miles to where they lived (on Big Willow Creek) in Henderson County. My father had sent her word through the lines to come to him if she could get there, if she brought nothing except the children and what they had on their backs. So she had sold and given away all she had and was on her way to Knoxville, Tennessee, to the "Yankees."

Now, when she told me where she had started I was amazed. I

was almost speechless for a moment to think of my condition. My Husband gone to the Yankees and my mother started. It was near sundown when they came. I said; "Mother I am going with you, for we will all starve or be killed here." She said: "Mary, I am not going to tell you to go or to stay, for I don't know what will happen to us before we get through; though I would be glad of your company."

Now you may guess I did not sleep much, for my thoughts ran fast. I just had until daybreak to make up my mind. When morning came, I had made up my mind to go. Father-in-law said: "Mary, you can't go; you will take that baby away and starve him to death."

I said: "Yes I will go. My husband is there and my mother is going, and the 'Rebs' will starve us to death, and what do I want to stay here for?"

Father-in-law left the house; he could not bear to see me start. Mother said: "Now Mary, if you go with us I will make a pilot out of you, for you have more tongue than I." So we started up the river through the rough country called the Pinkbed Mountain, and traveled one day in that direction. But we made only about eight or nine miles, for we came to the river and had no way to cross except to wade. We all sat down on the bank and pulled off our shoes and waded, thinking that a rough job; put on our shoes again and traveled about one mile when we came to the river again; pulled off and waded again, and so on until we crossed that river eight times, though we quit pulling off our shoes, we went in shoes and all.

We arrived at Luke Osteen's (Pink Beds area) just at dark. Next day it rained all day, and we had to stay another day and night. They told us there that we could not get through the mountains with all those children. That almost put us out of heart; but we started back the next morning and were told how to go to keep from wading the river and how to go to the left of Asheville to keep from being taken up by the Confederate soldiers.

We came back in two miles of my father-in-law's about sundown and stayed at George Orr's that night. My father-in-law heard we were there and he was not satisfied. He came by sunup next morning to see if I was in the notion to go back. He came in at the gate as I was at the pump washing my face. He said: "Mary, are you going back?" "No sir," I said, "I didn't start to go back. I am going to Knoxville if I don't starve or get killed on the way." My little boy just nineteen months old ran up to him, for he thought a heap of his grandfather. "Well Mary," said my father-in-law, "I don't want any hardness; but if you will go, you shall not take this child:" and he picked up the child as he said it. I cannot tell you what I felt. If you have a child, think how you would feel if some one should step up to you and say, "You shall not have it any longer unless you follow me."

I begged and cried until George Orr, at whose house we had spent the night, ran through the hall into the kitchen to keep me from hearing him. I went to the kitchen where he was and asked him to go to my father-in-law and take the child from him. He said no, he would have nothing to do with it. As I went back to the gate, his wife said to me, "Mary, there are enough of you to take it from him." So I started and asked mother to come and help me. Father-in-law ran down the road and I thought he was gone. I fell at the gate and begged and cried until the child got scared and began crying too. The old man could not stand that; he put the child down, and it ran back to me and put its little arms around my neck to make me quit crying. The old man said, "I would not have put it down if I had not thought you would be fool enough to kill yourself."

George Orr told us to go right to Asheville. The sun was about an hour high when we got there, and before we had time to think where we were, we ran right up on the Rebel guards and they halted us. I was scared almost to death, but tried to hold up my head. I asked them where Col. Palmer was. They pointed to a flight of stairs on the left and said that his office was there. We all strolled up the steps and got to the door. There were four or five men around in the room, writing. I asked where Col. Palmer was. They said he would be up in a minute. He came and we told our business, that we wanted a pass to go to Knoxville. Palmer said; "What in the hell do you want to go there for?" I told him we were going to get something to eat. He then asked where our men were; and I thought we were gone up. I had two brothers in the crowd, twelve and fourteen years old and large for their age; and the Confederates had already taken the sixteen year old boys, and I was afraid my brothers would be taken.

As I have said, my husband, Robert F. Orr, ran away from the "Rebs" in the spring; and soon after that, Folk's battalion was captured by the Yankees. So I told Palmer that Folk's battalion had been captured in that seizure. So they began to count us. The little children, tired out, were all huddled down on the floor. He counted us over twice and said: "I reckon I will have to let you go; it will take a heap of corn to feed these little children." He turned round to one of his men and said: "John, write a pass for Mrs. Middleton, three grown daughters and eight children."

You may guess I felt free when I got our pass. I took it in my hand and felt like a bird let out of a cage. By this time it was near sundown, and the next problem was where we were going to stay all night. When we came out on the street, some one told us there was a man by the name of Mathers that they thought we could stay with; he lived half a mile to the right of Asheville. So we marched double quick until we got there. Mother and the children stayed at the edge of the yard while I went up to the door and asked if we could stay all night.

"How many are there?" Mrs. Mathers asked. "Twelve", I said. "Oh, no; I can't keep so many." I turned to go, thinking that we were bound to stay out that night when she called me and said: "What is your name?" I said," "My names Orr, mother's name is Middleton." She jumped out at the door and said: "Hold on. What Middleton? It's not Kinston's wife, if it?" I said, "Yes." Mother stepped in the yard. Mrs.. Mathers threw her arms around mother's neck and said: "Why, Sis, you know I will let you stay, if we have to lie on the floor."

Though they were "Rebs", I was never better treated in my life; and they did not charge us a cent. Mr. Mathers also told us that Palmer was bound to give us something to eat if we asked for it; so we sent my two brothers back to him and got a supply of such as he had, - corn meal, and rice and salt; and he said if we would wait until noon we could have some beef.

But we did not wait. We carried our corn down to Madison County and swapped it for flour. We tried to keep a little rations on hand all the time, so when we came to a place where they would not give us anything to eat and would let us stay in the house, we would cook our own rations. We were two days going from Asheville to Marshall. We stayed one night at a Mrs. Bailey's. There was man in Marshall who took us for tramps; but, although we were nothing but a crowd of women and children, we surely made him know better. After he found out that we were not to be fooled with, he seemed to be very sorry for us and wanted to help us, but we were so angry with him we would not have any of his help.

We traveled about eight miles next day; and when night came we were five miles from where anyone lived. We knew we would have to lie out that night, and we had nothing to eat except a piece of bread about the size of my hand for each of us. There was a little house on the other side of the river; the river was on one side of the road, but we could not get to the house. We came to a patch of corn. I said: "Mother, we never have stolen anything yet; but now here is a corn patch and we will have some roasting ears." So we got over the fence and got one ear apiece, which made twelve in all. I felt mean about it, for maybe the corn belonged to some very poor man. There was a house about two hundred yards from the corn patch, and no one lived in it; so we took our headquarters there that night, all wet from the rain that fell that day. Mother had a few matches in her pocket. We struck all of them but one, and no fire. At last I took our pass out of my pocket and got the paper it was wrapped in and got fire with it from the last match. We all had a suit of clothes besides the ones we had on. We put them under our heads and lay on the floor and kept fire all night.

Next morning we traveled until two or three o'clock in the afternoon, when we came to some one's house and got something to eat. We thought we were now among strangers; but the woman asked us who we were and where we were going; and when I told her mother's name, she said: "Why, Sis, is that you?" We sure had a little meeting. She was one of mother's schoolmates.

We had to show our pass at Big Ivey. It was the only time we were asked to show it. We got within one or two miles of the Paint Mountain, and it rained the hardest rain I think I ever saw fall. We came to a house after we had got awfully wet, and we thought we would go in till the rain stopped. We went in the hall, not seeing any one. Directly there came a woman with a pail of water, and I told her we thought we would stop a minute out of the rain. She never made any reply but began to wash the floor where our clothes dripped. We certainly got out of there. We got in the big road, and one of my sisters turned round at the gate and just preached their funeral until we had to make her stop. We didn't know what kind of people they were.

By this time the rain was over but the road was full of water. We got about one half mile away from that house when we looked back and saw four men on horses coming from the direction of that house as hard as they could. I said, "We are gone up now." I knew it was Rebs. I told my sister to hold her tongue now, for that was why those Rebs were coming after us. The halted us and asked us where we were going, and we told them, They said, "Haven't you mail, carrying through?" We said, no. They said: "We must search you, for we have heard lots of people say no, and have found lots of mail with them." So they got off their horses and searched our bundles and the little boys' pockets, and went back.

We soon got to Paint Creek, and "it was up." We were already wet, and we packed up the least children and waded up to our waist in water. We crossed Paint Mountain that evening and stayed that night with a man at the foot of the mountain. They were Rebs, but they treated us very well, though we could see that they did not like us. It was hot weather. We went to bed, our clothes all wet, and got up the next morning, put on our wet clothes and started again.

We traveled until about one o'clock, when it came another rain as big as ever. This time we stopped before it began to rain. Oh, what a rain. It washed away fences and everything as it went. We had to stay there all night. They were very poor people; they could not furnish us any beds to lie on, or anything to eat except roasting ears. We gave them forty cents for one dozen roasting ears and slept on the floor. They gave us wood to keep a fire all night, and about midnight fire popped out on me and burned through my clothes. You may guess I woke, and did not sleep much more.

Next morning we started bright and early on our journey. The road was filled with logs and brush, so we had to travel slowly to get along. We almost got out of heart for five or six miles. Next we came to the mouth of the Chucky River. We had to cross it in a canoe. I thought we were at the end of the journey, for I knew we would get drowned. Some of us had never been in a canoe, but we knew we had to do something, so I began to holloa over.

It was about half an hour before any one came. At last an old Negro woman came and said she could not take us all at once, so I took my child and three of my brothers and sisters and went over all right. I felt safe myself; but when I looked to the other side my heart ached for fear some of us would be left in the water. The old Negro got about half way over the next time and ran against a snag of some sort which threw her in the river; but she grabbed the side of the canoe and bounced in and grabbed the pole and went to the other side all right and brought the rest across.

We felt as if we had been let out of jail, and went our way rejoicing. We traveled about two miles when we heard some one shout. We looked behind on the side of the hill in the woods and saw six men coming on horseback at full speed. They came up and spoke to us and asked where we were going. We said we were going to Knoxville. They said; "Go on; we will soon be there too." And on they went. They turned off to the left after they passed us, so we thought we were free again.

We stayed at a rich man's house the next night, two miles from Morristown. He did not want us to stay, but we begged him. We told him we did not want to stay out, and we would do our own cooking if he would let us have the use of his cooking vessels, and we would sleep on the floor. So they said we could stay. We lay on the carpet that night. They were "Rebs" and did not have much to say to us.

Next morning we traveled a short distance when we saw four men coming toward us. I said, "Mother, I believe that's Yankees." Sure enough, when they came up they asked where we were from, and we told them from North Carolina. One of them said, "I told you so." They asked us where were going and we told them and they all waved their hats and wished us good luck. We asked them if they were Yankees. They said they were, and we told them we were not afraid of them as we had been of the "Rebs" we saw the day before. They said we need not fear any more now, for we were in Yankeedom.

I cannot describe my feelings; I felt so relieved I felt safe. We aimed to take the train at Morristown; but when we got there, there had been a big battle at Knoxville, and the Rebs had lost, and as they fled back up the railroad they tore up the crossties and piled them in heaps and set them afire, and they were still burning when we got to Morristown. You may guess that was a sight for us, for we had never seen a railroad before, - and then to see it burning and knock us out of our ride.

We walked the railroad track to Flat Creek, within thirteen miles of Knoxville. The train ran to Flat Creek; that was as far as it could go.

I forgot to state at the outset that my mother sold all that she had for Confederate money, except one cow that she sold for $15 in silver. She gave $3 of that for a ride to Knoxville from Flat Creek.

We stayed all night at Flat Creek. Next morning we were all anxious to see the train coming. We went out to the station, and the train came, and we were all in as soon as it was good stopped, for they told us it would not stop long. The little boys, my brothers, were so taken off with the sight that they ran from one window to the other until the train whistled, and then such a scared set you never saw. They started for their seats and fell down as they went.

I have talked of being out of heart on our way; but we never really got out of heart until then. My father had gone to the Yankees; but, instead of going in the army as my husband did, he rented a farm in three miles of Knoxville and made a crop of corn, beans, molasses and such; and we aimed to go to him. But there we were in Knoxville and knew not which road to go to find him. We went three miles on several roads. We asked everybody we met on the street, till I got ashamed to ask any more, if they knew any one by the name of Middleton. At last, near night, one man told us to go to the provost marshal and he would tell us what to do. So we went and found him, or at least his headquarters. They told us there that we would have to prove our loyalty before we could get anything.

We told him that there was no one here that we knew until we could find father. So he wrote on a piece of paper and handed it to us and told us to go to the relief society and give that to them and they would give us something to eat. He showed us where to go. We went. They read the paper and we told them we had just come and did not know where to go. They gave us some flour, rice, sugar, salt, coffee and soda and told us to go to the Bell house on Main Street, which had one hundred rooms in it, and we would find a vacant room and could occupy it.

We went and found the room; and the rest of the house was filled with what they called "refugees." One woman met us at the door and found out what we wanted. She said; "What the devil do you want to come here for? This is the nastiest place I ever saw in my life. They have whooping cough, measles, mumps, and everything that's nasty."

We turned round and sat down on a bench by the well in the edge of the yard. It was nearly sundown. I could not bear to go in. Mother and I began to cry, and two soldiers stepped up to us and seemed to be sorry for us and asked us what was the matter. We told them we were not used to staying in such a hole as that. They told us it was so near night they could not do anything for us; but if would stay there till morning, they knew of a house about a half-mile from there they could get for us. So we stayed.

Next morning these soldiers come and told us they had been and got a room in that house and they went with us and loaned us two blankets to use a while. I felt like I was at home with Yanks camped all around us, and every store house full of goods. We had left our little town, Hendersonville, empty, not a yard of cloth nor a pound of coffee nor anything else in it, and not much to eat in the country, nobody to make anything except women and children. I concluded at last to advertise for Father, so I wrote a little piece and took it to the printing office.

We stayed there five days. One day there came a man and said he heard we were from North Carolina and thought we might be some of his neighbors; but we were not. I told him my husband's name, he said he knew him; said his tent was joining his at Cumberland Gap. The man said his name was Henderson and he was discharged from the army on account of bad health; and he told me where to write. So I wrote a letter that night. He also told me where I might find Father.

One of my sisters and I started next morning to find him. We went through Knoxville and asked for a pass to get out of town. They told me it was against orders to give any one a pass without proving their loyalty. I told them my condition and begged for a pass until they gave me one. We went two miles out on the Maryville Road and inquired for Middleton. Mrs. Dial, the woman of the house where we stopped, said to her grandson, "Well, aint that the man's name that stayed here last night?" He said that it was and that he was looking for his family. My sister and I jumped from our seat and spring to the door and said, "That's Father." Mrs. Dial grabbed us by the arm and said, "Hold on. Is this some of his family?" We said Yes; and she would not let us go on but made her grandson saddle the horse and go after him. While he was gone she fixed dinner for us; but we could not eat much for crying with joy that the lost was found.

Father came back on the horse, and Will walking. When they got in hearing of us he called out. My sister and I knew his voice and we went to the gate; and I looked back and Mrs. Dial was coming too, the tears running down her cheeks. She threw her hands up and shouted, "Oh, Mr. Middleton, I must rejoice with you, for the lost is found. You seemed so badly out of heart last night I was sorry for you; and now I am glad I can help you rejoice."

We then went back to Knoxville, and you may guess we had a meeting when we got to Mother and the rest of the children. We had heard straight news from Robert F., and found Father. Though we had not a bed to sleep on, nor a chair to sit on, nor a table to eat on, nor a quilt to cover us except the two blankets of our own and the two those soldiers loaned us, we felt happy, not thinking how we were going to live hereafter.

Father rented a house near his crop, within two miles of Knoxville, and I drew rations out of Knoxville until the war closed.

We were two weeks and four days on the road. We stayed two days at one place near Morristown and washed up our clothes. We all had two suits with us. There were two almost babies to carry and our bundles, which made our trip wearisome.

My two younger sisters were lively and would laugh at Mother and me for looking so sad on the way. I would get out of heart sometimes and almost wish I had not started. Then, the thought of living in the Confederacy and being in dread of my life, they knowing my husband was with the Yankees or in the mountains (they did not know which), would make me go to the Lord in prayer, asking Him to guard us through, which I truly believe He did. Then I would travel on a day or two in good heart with the thought of getting where we would be protected.

It was the fifth day of September, 1864, that we found father. He then took us to Col. John Baxter who vouched for our loyalty, which set us all right.

In the winter of 1864 my father moved twenty miles below Knoxville and stayed there till the close of the war. In March, 1865 my husband came home sick and stayed until the first of August when he went to his command and was mustered out, I believe, on August 18th.

Then we were free to battle through life the best we could. All we had before he started to the war was gone, we knew not where. We had to commence anew with two children. But the war was over and our life saved, and we would not complain. We stayed in Tennessee seven years, and we thought it best to come back to old North Carolina where he had a little piece of land all in the woods. He has built a house and opened a little farm and is living on it yet.

I am the mother of seventeen children, of whom eight are dead and nine are living. My health is gone down until I am not able to work much; and sitting about and studying over my life I just thought I would write out a sketch of my war life to let the younger generation know a little of the poor Southern woman's trials and hardships.

I can say we have tried to put our trust in the Lord, and He surely has been with us, or we could not have gone through with what we have. We truly think we are aided by the Master; for everybody told us before we started that we could not get through without being killed or taken up and put in jail. But somehow I did not fear at all, for I was so determined to go that I never thought of being afraid. I just said, "Where there's a will there's a way, and the Lord will provide." I have never regretted my trip.

Robert F. stayed in the Federal army two years. When he came home he was not the man he was before, though we have both done a lot of hard work, whether able or not, for that was and is yet all the way we had to support our family.

There is no one knows the trials and hardships of the Southern men and women, except those who endured it. For the Union men who would not fight for the Confederacy had to leave their families and risk their lives to go through the woods to the other side.

Robert F. Orr said he never fired but one gun while in the Confederate army and that was at a squirrel on a Sunday. I can say I have seen a sight of soldiers, - hundreds and thousands, - but never saw a badly wounded or dead soldier.

Although this story does not mention it, this family, like so many others, had divided loyalties. Mary's older brother James Wesley Middleton, served the Confederacy in Co "I" of the 16th NC and applied for a pension in 1905 while living in TN. Mary's brother-in-law, James F. Revis also served the Confederacy.

Civil War in the Mountains

CHAPTER 3
MOONSHININ' AND COOKIN'

"Every man is a quotation from all his ancestors."
-Ralph Waldo Emerson, 1803-1882
American Poet, Lecturer and Essayist.

Revenuers: Examining a Family Story
by Jerry Owen

The telling and retelling of oral family history stories sometimes creates a slightly distorted view of the actual truth of the matter. It then falls on the serious family historian as to how to proceed. Should the story just be allowed to continue on its merry way through time, being constantly distorted and embellished, or should the truth be sought and set forth? When my brother Danny Owen and I began our adventure into family history and genealogy, we chose the path of greater resistance and decided to challenge every oral family history story that we could get our hands on. We did this not out of any disrespect for our ancestors, especially not our Grandfather Owen since many of our stories originated from him, but rather out of a desire to set forth as true of a historical picture as we possibly could for all generations of our family to come.

The following story is a good example of how this process works, so I decided to explain the changes we had to make in an old family oral story in order to adhere more closely to the actual historical record. This is sometimes a very hard process since many families do not leave good written records, and the Owen family falls into that category. Hopefully you will see how this can be compensated for in this story.

Original Oral Family Story

It has been told for several years in our Owen family that my great-grandfather, William Sherman Owen, ran a fairly successful still in the mountains of Northeast Georgia and Southwest North Carolina. The story is that it was legal to brew whiskey in Georgia and illegal to brew it in North Carolina. At the same time it was legal to sell it in North Carolina and illegal to sell it in Georgia. I have thus far been unable to verify this part of the story, but what we have verified is that moonshine was distilled by one of our ancestors in the Georgia Mountains. The story goes on to say that he would brew it in Towns County, Georgia, walk across the state line which was all on the same mountain and sell it in Clay County, North Carolina. A pretty good little money-making operation at that.

Our Search for the True Story

We sifted through every official family document we could in seeking to verify this story. I personally traveled to Towns County, GA and Clay County, NC, visited the county courthouse in Towns County and talked with some old timers from Towns County via email. I actually went to the old Owen family log cabin where my Grandfather Jesse Owen was born. One part of the story becomes easily verified. The Owen home did sit on a mountain that includes both states. Looking through land documents and wills paints a slightly different version of the story. Without going into a lot of legal jargon, we found this handwritten statement in a legal document giving a description of the parameters of the Owen property, the original written words are "from a large white Oak down to the creek by where WJ Owens used to still before the revenue took it away" The WJ Owens mentioned would have had to be my 2nd great-grandfather, William Jackson Owen, father of William

Mountains in Towns County, Georgia

Sherman Owen.

This began to cast an entirely new light on the situation. We interviewed an older family relative, my great aunt who lived in Bonham, Texas at the time. She was the last living child of William Sherman Owen. Her name was Maude Ballard Owen and she was 96 at the time. She has since passed away and is buried in Bonham. Her mother had always told her that her grandfather was an outlaw and was always being hunted by the law, but she did not know why. Her grandfather would have been William Jackson Owen. After that we began looking for a photo of William Jackson Owen and found out that he would never allow anyone to take a photo of him under any circumstances. Apparently he did not want his face to be recognizable. We learned there were reasons stretching back to his Civil War experiences that also played into this desire not to be identified. There are several photos of William Sherman so it would seem he did not feel a need to hide his face from the law. Armed with both the written record of his still and with family oral corroboration, we arrived at the conclusion that the family history story we had heard for so long was about the wrong man. William Sherman Owen had his faults, but he was not guilty in this instance. We have therefore changed the story to its truest form as follows. May God have mercy on our souls and may WJ & WS Owen both forgive us if we are wrong!!

WJ Owen and the Revenuers

During the late 1870's and early 1880's it was very difficult to make a decent living for your family living in the mountains unless you had some way to supplement your income. William Jackson Owen, who we will call by his nickname Jackie from this point on, and his wife Elizabeth Jane Owen already had nine children by this time and would eventually have two more. Jackie already had reasons that kept him uneasy around the authorities relating back to his involvement in the Civil War, but that is another story altogether.

During this period of time Jackie set up a still on the banks of a fast flowing creek in Towns County, GA in the area of Upper Bell Creek. Jackie was a very good distiller of whiskey and his product was very much in demand both in Georgia and North Carolina. The manufacture of whiskey was a family tradition with the Owens that had come down through many generations. Jackie's father James and his Grandfather John W. Owen had both manufactured their own whiskey for their own special uses for as long as Jackie could remember. He had heard stories about ancestors even farther back in history, even back in the old countries, who had this special gift, so it only seemed natural to him to take this talent and use it to feed his family. Unfortunately the laws of the Federal government and the state laws did not support this view. The Federal government had many years previously, during the time of the first American president George Washington, passed the hated Whiskey tax. Individuals such as Jackie who set up and operated stills to feed their families were persecuted and prosecuted. The simple act of providing for a man's family would make an outlaw out of him. The one thing Jackie had going for him was a quirk in state laws that made it less likely for him to be jailed for his activities. In Georgia he could run his still and as long as he did not try to sell the whiskey he was not breaking the law. He could go across into North Carolina and sell the whiskey, and it was not illegal as long as he did not distill it there.

The only catch to this plan was that it was against a federal law to transport it from one state to another state. Therefore he had to be extremely careful of his journeys from state to state, even though the two states met on the side of a mountain that belonged to the Owen family on both sides. All of Jackie's whiskey runs had to be nocturnal and through secret back trails that crisscrossed these mountains. These trails had been originally used by Cherokee Indians for many, many years. The Owen family had befriended many of these Cherokee and helped hide a few during the Cherokee removal, even though James Owen had been with the North Carolina Militia that helped remove the Cherokee to Oklahoma. It has been suggested that James used his service in the Militia to make sure his friends were not mistreated by the other white soldiers. What is known for sure is that once James was living in Towns County, Georgia some of the Owen family Cherokee friends lived in the same mountains. These Cherokee friends had shown Jackie all the old trails and this valuable knowledge became very important to Jackie's moonshine activities.

It was so exasperating to the authorities that at one point a plot was hatched between the Georgia and North Carolina sheriffs working in conjunction with the federal revenue officers to set an ambush for him. They had been tipped off by a local neighbor who did not care for Jackie but had befriended him in order to gain his confidence as to which trail he would be taking on one particular run. The two sheriffs and two federal revenue officers lay in wait on both sides of the state lines in order to catch him transporting the whiskey across the lines.

Jackie, however, had also inherited another trait from his Owen ancestors. He was extremely intuitive and sensed something was not right about this night. He therefore altered his path from the original plan and took a precarious and circuitous route over the more steep and rocky side of the mountain. On this trail there were places where every step was dangerous and few people other than Cherokee had ever taken it. All these old Cherokee trails were made for single file travel.

The sheriffs and the two revenuers waited all night but, when the sun began to come up, they realized they had been tricked again and became very angry. They sought out the informer and made him lead them to Jackie's still where they used large pick axes to demolish and dismantle the entire thing, making an end to Jackie's business and making life in the mountains a little harder for people just trying to survive.

This was the end of Jackie's still in Towns County, but not the end of his entrepreneurial ways. It was also not the last raid made by the two revenuers. They made another raid along with a third peace officer shortly after this on another prominent family in the same area. All three wound up buried under a smokehouse and are still there till this day. But that's another story for another time. This last bit of the puzzle and the violent end of the revenuers was related to me by a direct descendant of this family. For now I feel it wise and prudent that the name of this family remain undisclosed until such time as they themselves might choose to share this information.

SAVED FROM THE REVENUERS
by Winnie Owen Kropelnicki

On his way home from the war, John Owen found a small black child crying in the bushes. He took this child home, and he and his wife, Malinda, raised him just like he was one of their own. They named this boy Pete Owen, and Pete was well loved by all of his Owen brothers and sisters. Many Owen family stories involve Pete. This is one of those stories. It takes place in the wild mountains of the Gloucester Valley, deep in Owen country, in Transylvania County, North Carolina.

After Pete had grown to manhood, married and begun a family of his own, he would always return to the old Owen home at least one time each year to brew the family's yearly whiskey. Pete had perfected the art of whiskey brewing, and John preferred Pete's above all others.

The Owen family used this whiskey for many purposes. Each year Malinda would take a portion of it and cook up what she called the Spring Bitters. This is something she had learned from her grandmother. Not having access to local pharmacies such as we do today, these Spring Bitters served a wide range of medicinal purposes. She would also make a very strong cough syrup from the whiskey and a few other local ingredients. John always kept some of the whiskey on hand in case of visitors. This was his social drink of choice.

Close by the Owen home off in the mountains was a waterfall by the name of Stillhouse Falls. This was the location where John and Pete had their equipment for brewing whiskey. On one such occasion, John had made a neighbor angry and so the neighbor turned him in for operating the still. The neighbor told the sheriff when Pete was busily at his brewing work. The sheriff and one other man, perhaps a deputy or maybe even a revenuer, sneaked up on Pete and arrested him. They tied Pete's hands behind him and began to escort him out of the mountains.

In the meantime, one of the other neighbors had told John what was going on. In order to get Pete safely out of the mountains the sheriff had to walk him down through a deep rut that had been slowly created over the years by men and horses walking the same trail and the rains washing it out even deeper, so that it was a fairly deep trail with an embankment on both sides. The sheriff was walking along in the front followed by the other man who had one end of the rope in his hands. Just as they walked around a sharp turn in the trail, suddenly the sheriff found himself staring down the barrel of a big old shotgun.

The first words that came out of John were "loose that man". John was himself well versed in the law and acted in the official capacity of Justice of the Peace in those mountains. So he told the sheriff, "You have absolutely no business here; this man is making this whiskey for my own personal use". The sheriff at first tried to argue the point, but John was in no mood to argue. He said to the sheriff, "Take a good look down this barrel and tell me what you see." The sheriff stared into the gun barrel for a couple of minutes and responded. "All I see is darkness." Then John told him. "If I ever see you around here again, this darkness is the last thing on earth you will ever see".

According to Owen family oral history, they never saw that sheriff around there again, and John and Pete continued to brew excellent whiskey at Stillhouse Falls for many more years.

Sunday Dinner--
Sweet Potato and Possum Pie
by Jerry Owen

My Grandfather Owen used to tell this story. When he lived with his family in the beautiful majestic mountains of Towns County, GA sometime around the turn of the century, his Uncle Sam Owen was just a young man in his early twenties who became a school teacher. Sam lived with his brother, William Sherman Owen, my great-grandfather and family on the weekends and would travel across the mountains back to Clay County, NC to teach in a little one room log school house during the week. It took a while to make this trip in those days, so he would stay at the school during the week.

My Great-grandmother Sarah was very proud of her young brother-in-law. She wanted her boys to spend as much time with him as possible in the hopes this aptitude for knowledge and the good life would rub off on them and hopefully keep them from getting involved in moonshine or other rowdy things. She was a very religious woman and would not allow any spirits or foul language around her home.

Sarah was always really excited when the weekend would approach and would send the older boys out to fetch a healthy possum. According to my grandfather, her exact instructions were to go and find her the fattest, best looking possum they could find and woe to them if they returned with a scrawny, skinny one. She was also a strict disciplinarian and the boys had reason to take her seriously.

Once she had the right possum she would dress it out, place it in her big iron pot, surround it with lots of sweet potatoes and slowly simmer it on a low flame for a few hours. My granddad said that the aroma that would begin to fill the house was so good that it actually made your mouth begin to water. By the time Sam was there and Sunday dinner was on, everyone was so hungry and worked up that possum and sweet potato pie did not last very long. She was apparently quite well known in the mountains for this because one of the problems was once Sunday came it was hard to keep other family and friends from suddenly showing up for Sunday Dinner uninvited!!!

Mountain Food Stories
by Gordon Owen

Since I was born near Akron and grew up near Cleveland, my "mountain food" stories have more to do with what my parents liked and did than actually being in the mountains. Of course, we had quart jars of sourwood honey from Grandpap's hives in Balsam Grove, NC and every trip to the mountains meant bringing back a couple bottles of Dukes mayonnaise and several gallons of what my mother called "water worth drinking."

For that matter, squirrel, woodchuck, and pheasant harvested in Ohio and venison harvested in Pennsylvania probably taste about like genuine mountain food. From as recently as a week ago, I can vouch that redeye gravy (black coffee quickly heated and stirred in the pan you just used to fry several pieces of ham) tastes as good in California as it does elsewhere.

Once upon a time in Olmsted Falls, Ohio, the Birdseye Food Company (i.e., orange juice) was sponsoring a contest for elementary schoolchildren. For each student, the teacher assigned daily points for how nearly the kid's breakfast came to the ideal in providing a balanced diet. Turns out that a particular fourth-grade teacher named Mrs. Wright didn't know how to score a breakfast of deep fried salt pork, gravy, and biscuits.

I never cared much for groundhog meat despite my father's encouragement. Doctor once explained to my mother his novel theory that once a child is big enough to open the refrigerator door, the parents are no longer responsible for how fat their child becomes. Turning to me, he began to explain that in making my food choices I should emphasize vegetables and lean, red meat. Not being shy even as a five-year-old, I interrupted with "But, Doctor, I don't like groundhog."

Thanks to me, conversation in the teachers' lounge and at the medical center must have addressed the sociological implications of mountain folk moving north after WWII.

Grandmother Mary Lee
by April Montgomery

Life was not easy for my Grandmother Mary Lee, as a child. She told me the story of baking her first apple pie and needing a crate to stand on to use the stool. She accidentally put salt in that first apple pie, rather than sugar. Mary Lee was just six years old when her mother died and left her to watch after 4 year old J W, and 2 year old Vernon.

It was not long before Mary Lee's father remarried and the family once again began to grow. Mary Lee completed the sixth grade and was then sent to work to help provide for the family. She always talked about picking cotton.

One particularly hot day, Mary Lee had completed her day's work in the cotton field and was walking home when she ran across a still. Being 14 years old, she was plenty old enough to know what it was and more than big enough to work the still.

It was so hot. She was so tired and thirsty. She didn't think one drink would hurt anything. So she began to drink. It was so sweet. Watermelon. She kept drinking, unaware at how quickly strong alcohol would affect her on an empty stomach.

Her walk home was not so pleasant. More than once she found herself face down in the ditch after a short tumble. It was the only time she ever admitted to having a strong drink.

Possum Hunting
by John Turner

Never ate possum but did trap some in a rabbit box by accident (what a surprise I got next morning). Also went on possum hunts with a man named Foster who lived in our neighborhood and who always had a gaggle of us guys hanging around.

One night in particular, he told me to shinny up that tree (must have been over thirty feet up) and run the possum out since he wouldn't come down. I got up there and started shaking the tree and that possum came straight down in my face. We tried to see who would hit the ground first. I did and he landed on top of me. Them things are mean and I think he won that round. The dogs and Foster got the best of him though.

I also had to go and collect polk sallet for my aunt. She loved that stuff. Never gave me any even though I always wondered what it tasted like. I also had a great aunt who used to have me collect little green plants with yellow flowers on them. She would brew them up for tea.

Now, this was in Greenwood County, SC and during my young years of about 12 -16. Did hunt and eat rabbit and squirrel though. Too many little bones, but done right, they're good.

The Beans Burned
by Saorise

I remember my Grandmother saying that there was going to be a storm 'cuz her beans burned or they almost burned.

Sure enough, the rain would start.

Later I found that she was right, that instead of being an old wives tale, this one is scientifically proven.

As the barometric pressure drops, water will come to a boil quicker and boil away faster.

So all of our Grans were weather women!!

Course I didn't learn how smart she was till she was gone. As teens we all have a tendency to put down the things told to us by our grandparents. Now I have spent the last 20 years trying to figure out her recipe for "stack cake". I got the creamed potatoes down, but that stack cake has eluded me for years.

BUTTERMILK TRAIL
by Jerry Owen

In 1908 my great-grandfather, William Sherman Owen, made the decision to move his family from the mountains of Towns County, GA to Grayson County, Texas. This decision was made because he believed from correspondence with a cousin of his already in Texas that he could make a lot of money in the cotton business. At the time it was very hard to support his family there in the mountains, and he had resorted to making moonshine to supplement his income. Only problem was, he constantly had to dodge the authorities. His wife my great-grandmother, Sarah Elizabeth Rhodes Owen, was a very religious woman and hated the idea of her children growing up being exposed to the moonshine business.

He sold his land on the side of a mountain for $300, which was quite chunk of money then. They loaded the family up in a wagon and packed only the necessary things and headed across the mountains towards Murphy, NC, which was the nearest place to catch the train to Texas. Before leaving Sarah baked several large cornpones and made several gallons of buttermilk. This was to be the family's food on the long trip to Texas. It took a couple of days and nights just to get through the mountains to Murphy from Hiawassee and one thing they didn't count on was the effect of the damp air on the cornpone. Apparently by the time they reached Murphy it had turned green and so they had to dispose of it at the train station. This left only the buttermilk which they had plenty of for the next three days and nights on the train.

At the time my grandfather Jesse Luon Owen was only eight years old and he loved buttermilk, so he was constantly asking for more buttermilk. Invariably as he would take a drink of buttermilk the train would lurch or hit a bump. He was constantly spilling buttermilk on his clothes. My great-grandmother was a very fastidious woman and always scolded him each time this happened and made him clean up. The older children thought this was pretty funny and so they all named the journey the Buttermilk Trail. That name stuck and so now, anytime any one of our various Owen family members makes the trip back to Hiawassee, we always refer to it as the Buttermilk Trail. My grandfather made at least two trips back there, once in 1964 with my Aunt Fredna and once in 1967 with me. Each time he would always buy buttermilk all along the way in honor of the Buttermilk Trail.

CHILDHOOD MEMORIES
by Mary McPherson

Polk Sallet... you pare boil it several (4 or 5) times, draining off the water each time, this gets rid of the poisons in the sallet; then you put it in a skillet, bacon drippings is the best, stir fry plain, or with scrambled eggs, not bad, not bad. Would love to have some of Mom's today!

We all are raised different, and those of us who had the gift from God to let us learn to live off the land, were the richest! The generations coming along, will never have what I had, I'm sad! Went blackberry picking, wild blueberry picking, went swimming in the favorite swimming hole in the creek (now wouldn't dare due to all the dye that a factory put in the creek); fished, trot-lined fished with my dad. We did that all night; we had a trailer behind his tractor, and we curled up in a sleeping bag, and checked the trotlines several times in the night; used to come home with tubs of fish! Those days are gone now, how much treasure we've lost...

MOONSHININ'
by April Montgomery

It has always been told that my grandfather, J.B. Giles, brewed and ran moonshine in the 1950's. It has been passed down that he even had a still on the sheriff's property for many years without being found. When J.B. met my grandmother, Mary Lee Jackson, she already had 6 children. To provide for a large family, my Granny had to have her part in the "business" as well.

Being tipped off that the police were on their way to the family's home, my Granny would hide the moonshine. It was recalled that she would hide it in the washing machine as well as putting the kids to bed and putting the jugs under the covers with them. If my Granny hid the 'shine... the police never found it.

If J.B. had a hand in stashing it away... 98% of the time, the result was him being hauled off to jail.

My Granny also had a sense about when J.B. would be caught. My aunt recalled J.B. leaving to make a run once and Granny standing on the porch. A few minutes later, Granny came in saying "Well, they got him".

July Supper

by Sam Owen

This was a family tradition passed down from my ancestors, the Owen and Galloway folks from the wilds of Wolf Mountain, NC, the home of my 2nd great-grandfather, Andrew Jackson Owen.

At dawn, put 6-8 cups snapped beans in a crock pot, turn on high. Fry up a half pound of salt pork. Right before it browns throw in 2 chopped onions. Fry till onions are soft. Dump everything in crock pot, grease and all. Add water to cover. This will be yer "pot likker". At noon; adjust salt and pepper to taste and turn to "low". Add some quartered new potatoes.

Make peach cobbler: Butter a 9x12 dish and add a double layer of peeled, quartered peaches, sprinkle with brown sugar, cinnamon and chopped pecans. Top with dumpling dough. Sprinkle a little more brown sugar. Bake at 350 'till brown and bubbly (about 35-40 min). Best served warm or at room temp with vanilla ice cream.

4 pm, make corn pone. (No sugar!) Beans should be done, check for salt. Slather pone with real butter. Pour cold buttermilk. Pass sliced 'maters and cukes. Spoon up them beans. Add quartered raw onions and hot peppers fer them that care fer 'em. Fried yaller squash. (Is this as close to Heaven, or what?). Fried okra if'n you

please. Don't expect much conversation for 'bout half an hour. When you hear the second or third groan, dish up yer cobbler with a scoop of ice cream.

So easy, yet so-o-o good!

CHAPTER 4
Healin', Dowsin' and Cauls

"Men go back to the mountains, as they go back to sailing ships at sea, because in the mountains and on the sea they must face up, as did men of another age, to the challenge of nature. Modern man lives in a highly synthetic kind of existence. He specializes in this and that. Rarely does he test all his powers or find himself whole. But in the hills and on the water the character of a man comes out."

-Abram T. Collier

Healing, Dowsing, and Cauls
by Kathy Owens

There are still a few around the Pickens, SC area that are thrush doctors and such. Mrs. Hendricks was the best thrush doctor until she died. The sad fact is that people's faith is not what it used to be and that makes a difference. People tend to look at you as if you're from another planet.

My dad was an herbalist; he also took out fire, and stopped blood. He was also a water dowser and found most of the wells at the resort near Table Rock. He has been dead for three years and folks still call my mom for different things, not knowing that he is gone. If any of you have the book Journey Home, a story about my dad is in the book. Several articles and his photo have appeared in the Greenville News.

I can also dowse for water. My husband was a skeptic until just before we married. I gave him a dowsing rod, showed him what to do, and it twisted the bark off in his hand. Needless to say, he is now a believer. I can't explain how a dowsing rod works, I don't have a clue, but it does.

About a caul: My mom and her twin sister were both born with a caul over their faces. The doctor told my grandmother that during that time, most doctors let the baby die, because they didn't know how to remove the caul. It is a thin skin and the baby will suffocate to death. The story is that a baby born with a caul over its face can "see" things, have visions and such. This is another "taboo" subject. It scares people to think that this could be true.

Mountain Healing
by Mary Ellen Yelton

My grandmother, Ollie Smith Hoyle, dipped snuff. When I was a child, every time one of her grandchildren got stung by a bee (and that was often; we NEVER wore shoes in the summer), she would take a pinch of snuff out of her mouth and place it on the bee sting, after making sure the stinger was out. It really worked to stop the swelling and the itching.

WART HEALING
by Saoirse

How many of our grandparents and great-grandparents would have shuddered and started praying at the very mention of anything paranormal? Yet a lot of them experienced it in their daily lives. Most believed in omens: a bird in the house, a shoe on the bed, inch worm on your body.

They did a lot of things guided by the same thing our ancient ancestors were guided by, the moon. My Grandma wouldn't even have a tooth pulled without consulting the almanac for the phase of the moon and the position of the astrological signs and stars.

People used to bring their babies to grandpa for him to blow into their mouths to cure thrush. He is not a seventh son and he _did_ see his father, so probably he was born with a caul.

When I was 13, we went to visit the "old folks". I was a very sophisticated thirteen year old who knew all about science, etc (in my mind I was anyway) and thought new ways were best and old ways were just a crock. At the time I had a very large plantar wart and all its little seedlings on the bottom of my foot. I couldn't even wear a shoe. Pa told me he could take it off for me. So the big, bad, sophisticated 13 year old thought, sure, humor the old man and let him do his little thing. Well, he rubbed it with oil and said some words I couldn't understand then but now believe to be Celtic or Gaelic. In my mind I had a big laugh and then forgot about it. Three days later I took my socks off to warm my toes at the wood stove and the wart came off with it. Pa saw it, jumped up, grabbed it and said some more words and tossed it straight into the fire so it wouldn't come back. And, by the way, it never did.

WART CURING
by Mary McPherson

My husband tells a story about his warts. He had them real bad on his hands, and an ol' man came by and Mama Mc told him she didn't know what to do for them. The ol' man said he did. He handed her a nickel, and said something. Now throw the nickel away, where it will never be found, he told her. Apparently she hid it, and it wasn't found till after she died. After it was found, my husband's warts came back!

Also my Grandpa Turpin could conjure. My aunt had thrush and her baby had thrush in his mouth. He took the baby, said words over him, and the baby's thrush was cleared up by morning, and so was the mother's. My aunt asked my grandpa would he pass this gift down to her. He said, "No, you do not have enough faith."

MOUNTAIN MEDICINE
by Tammy Jernigan

My great-grandmother was named Ary. When some one was ill in the family, they would go and tell her. She would go into the woods and make some of the awfulest looking and smelling stuff for them, but it would always work and heal whatever their sickness was.

The story has been passed down that one of my great aunts did not want to have anymore children because the last one almost took her and the baby's life. Granny Ary made her some kind of tonic or tea every week to drink and she never got pregnant again.

Granny Ary was part Cherokee and a straight-talking woman; she always said what she thought no matter what it was. They always said she was a hard woman, but I guess in those days, there were a lot of bad things to get through.

CAULS
by Catherine Gage Wedge

My mother was born with a "caul" over her head. She was of Scots-Irish descent. She also had circles or rings of a different shade around the outside of her irises (colored part of the eye). Her maternal family from the mountains of NC told me that both these things meant she had the "second sight", that is, the ability to be psychic, seeing and knowing things beyond the normal range of our other five senses. I believe she was clairvoyant and telepathic, and I also believe that she could, under extreme circumstances, project her thoughts, to me at least. I experienced that on at least one occasion.

My grandmother, my mother's mother, born in the mountains of NC, also had "unusual" abilities. There is a mixture, most probably, of Cherokee in our line. This adds a whole other dimension to the ability to "step outside" of "normal" reality. However, I have never sought these things for their own sake, believing that they are to be treated with great reverence and respect. To say one uses them for the good is often a seductive line of reasoning. Enough to know that, in times of need, they seem to become active in me, too.

DOWSING
by Gordon Owen

I was 7 or 8 when my father taught me how to dowse. Nothing spooky here, just a practical way to avoid digging up the whole back yard when all you need is one hole to connect with a 220 line that's buried about 2 feet below the surface. Dad's technique used two pieces of bent welding rod, one held in each hand. I use two pieces of coat hanger wire, and I've learned not to use the spirally end where the coat hanger wire joined itself because it will cut open the palm of your hand when it twists.

Healin', Dowsin' and Cauls

Turns out that almost anybody can be taught to dowse, but it's easier if the person is of Welsh or Irish extraction. I take your left hand in my right hand while I hold the left wire, you hold the right one, and we walk forward. Once the wires twitch over a target, you know how to dowse. Once, with a French-German lady named Lorraine, I tried repeatedly, walking over a known target three or four times. Nothing happened. As we stepped back to try again, the wires twitched. Lorraine can now dowse, but only when walking backwards. Go figure.

CHAPTER 5
MOUNTAIN PEOPLE AND THEIR HISTORY

"I went to the woods because I wished to live deliberately, to front only the essential facts of life, and see if I could not learn what it had to teach, and not, when I came to die, discover that I had not lived."
-Henry David Thoreau, 1817-1862
American Essayist, Poet and Philosopher

LYNCH'S LAW
by Karen Patterson

American Revolutionary War soldier William Lynch from Pittsylvania Co., Virginia, distinguished himself both as a patriot and a militia man, providing both food to the Continental Army and militia service in the Battles of Guilford Courthouse, Haw River and Camden under General Nathaniel Greene.

Born in 1742, William Lynch served as a Delegate from Pittsylvania County to the Legislature in Virginia in the years of 1787 and 1788 with such notables as Patrick Henry and James Monroe.

On September 12, 1789, William Lynch and others, including Charles Lay, sent a Compact to the State Capitol stating; "Whereas, many of the inhabitants of Pittsylvania County, as well as elsewhere, have sustained great and intolerable losses by a set of lawless men who have banded themselves together to deprive honest men of their just rights and property, by stealing horses, counterfeiting and passing paper currency and committing many other species of villainy, too tedious to mention, and those vile miscreants do still persist in their diabolical practices, and have hereto escaped the civil power of impunity, it being almost useless and unnecessary to have recourse to our laws... we, the subscribers, being determined to put a stop to the iniquitous practices of those unlawful and abandoned wretches do enter into the following association..."

What this "association", known as the Lynch-men, pledged to do was take the law into their own hands, being remote and removed from more orderly systems of justice, and would round up the villains and thrash them with 39 lashes. Thus was the beginning of Lynch's Law.

What began as pioneer justice over 200 years ago by men of the frontier of our early nation unfortunately evolved into mob actions that are repugnant to all of decency. It is sorrowful to have the name of a great man, William Lynch, attached to the hangings and torture in times when we were not "removed from orderly justice."

By 1797, having obtained a land grant, William Lynch was in

residence in the Oolenoy Valley of the Pendleton District of South Carolina, where he raised six children by his second marriage on Jan 4, 1785, to wife Ann Moon, widow of Ashwell Stone.

William Lynch's descendents are abundant in Transylvania County, NC. Jason Gillespie, son of John Harvey Gillespie and Sallie Glazener, daughter of Abraham Glazener and Esther Beasley, married Elizabeth Lynch, who was the granddaughter of William Lynch, from his son Nathaniel Lynch, Sr. and wife, Sarah Jane Lay. And Jason's sister, Rebecca Gillespie married William "Fat Bill" Whitmire.

William and Rebecca Gillespie Whitmire had a son named George Washington Whitmire, who married Ary Jane Lynch, William Lynch's great-granddaughter, from grandson Bannister Lynch and his wife Frances Price, who was the daughter of Thomas Price and Ary Stewart Price.

G. W. Whitmire and Jane Lynch had daughters Emma, who married Lyman Culwell Galloway, and Rebecca, who married Coleman Columbus Galloway, both sons of Lyman Thayer Galloway and Selena Patterson.

Captain William Lynch died on July 15, 1820, and is buried on the old home place near the Oolenoy River, in Pickens, South Carolina

William Lynch's descendents have shown a proud heritage of Patriotism by serving their country in the War of 1812, War Between the States, WWI, WWII, Korea, Vietnam, Desert Storm, and the Gulf War.

PRANK STORY
by Kathy Owen

This prank was pulled 60 years or so ago.

One of my kinsmen worked in the cotton mill. As most of the workers did, he wore one pair of shoes to work and left his "working" shoes underneath his locker.

He purchased a new pair of shoes to wear to work, wore them in to the mill and removed them to put on his working shoes. When work time was over, he removed his working shoes and standing there, slipped on his new shoes. He started to walk and tipped over onto the floor. His feet wouldn't budge.

Slipping his feet out of the new shoes, he discovered that his new shoes had been nailed to the floor. Needless to say, he was NOT happy with his prankster friends or his new shoes. What people will do in the name of fun!

LITTLE RUF'S TRICK
by Linda Owen Anders

My dad, Arthur Tillman Owen, told me about how he helped my grandfather, Rufus William "Little Ruf" Owen, pull a prank on their neighbors. My dad said one evening at dusk my grandfather told him to come with him. My dad thought they were going to visit the neighbors, but just as they got in sight of the house, my grandfather told him to be quiet and slip off into the bushes. Rufus pulled out a spool of thin wire and, while my dad waited in the bushes, went up to the neighbor's porch and tied the wire around the porch post. He rolled the wire out as he returned and hid in the bushes with my dad.

Then he stretched the wire very tight and had my dad "pluck" on the wire. They could hear an eerie twang. The neighbor came to the door and looked out, saw nothing and went back inside. They waited a few moments and plucked the wire again. Again, the neighbor came to the door and this time came out onto the porch, looked around. He couldn't see anything so he shook his head and went back inside. My grandfather and my dad waited a few more moments and did the same thing. Once more, the neighbor came out with a puzzled look on his face.

Arthur Tillman "Slim" Owen

Finally, when they plucked the wire, the neighbor didn't even come to the door.

My grandfather and dad slipped back to the trail and started home. They had held in the laughter as long as they could! They stopped by the side of the trail and bent over double with laughter. When my grandfather could get his breath, he told my dad to go on home.

My grandfather went back to the neighbor's house and knocked on the door. He had to repeat his knock a couple of times before anyone came to the door. Finally, the neighbor opened the door a crack and then flung it open. He told my grandfather how they had been hearing a strange noise all evening and had finally decided it must be a ghost and the best thing for them to do was just stay in the house. My grandfather expressed his surprise and concern, went in the house and visited a little, and then left for home.

The neighbors never did find out that the "ghost" was two Owen men having a little fun, because my grandfather quietly undid the wire and took it home with him after bidding the family goodnight.

PEARSON AND AMANDA QUEEN OWEN
by Carolyn McCall Burgess submitted by Cynthia Burgess
(used with permission)

Richmond Pearson Owen was born February 25, 1895 on Wolf Mountain, Jackson County, North Carolina. He was the oldest son of James and Dovie Elizabeth Mathis Owen.

Pearson was raised on a farm and grew up knowing how to raise cattle, grow his own food, and make a living off the land. In those days, neighbors were few and far between, but just a few miles down the mountain lived a young couple, Wilburn and his young wife, Martha Owen Queen. When Pearson was twelve years old, he heard that the Queens had been blessed with the birth of their first child, daughter Amanda, on May 24, 1908.

Everybody was talking about this little girl, about what a pretty little thing she was. Pearson wanted to see this pretty baby, so one day he asked his father if he could go visit the Queens. In those day's children were not allowed to wander too far from home, but he was a good boy and had helped his father plant the cornfields and tend the cattle. Pearson's father said, all right son, but you be careful and don't stay too long.

So, off down the mountain went young Pearson. When he reached the cabin where the Queens lived, he told Martha that he had come to see her pretty little baby. The baby was lying in a handmade cradle by the fireplace. When Pearson looked down into her face, he said she looked just like a baby doll. Mandy had coal black hair, black eyes and a dark complexion. Pearson asked Martha if he could touch the baby, and he sat by the cradle for hours just holding her hand.

Pearson and Amanda Queen Owen

The day was passing fast and Pearson knew he had to get home before dark, but he just didn't want to leave that baby. He finally got up and told Martha that he had to get on home, and Martha told him to come back when he could to visit the baby. As Pearson walked to the door, he turned back to Martha and said, "You know, one of these days I'm going to marry that little girl."

On January 18, 1923 Pearson and his Baby Doll, Amanda 'Mandy' Queen were married in Owen's Gap by the Reverend Bowen. They had an outside wedding under the large oak trees in the gap. Several family members and friends attended; among them was Mandy's school teacher Beryl Morgan.

I talked with Miss Morgan 60 years later and she vividly remembered the day Pearson and Mandy were married. She told me how beautiful Mandy was on her wedding day. She wore a light blue dress and her long black hair hung down to her waist. Miss Morgan said after the ceremony Pearson picked Mandy up and sat her on the seat of his wagon, and they drove off together to set up housekeeping in a small cabin in Balsam Grove, North Carolina.

Pearson had a logging job in Balsam Grove, but after living there two years, he got to wanting to go back home. By this time their oldest child James Roland Owen was born. Pearson's father gave him twenty-six acres of land on Wolf Mountain, where he built a small cabin and made the land into a farm. This was very hard work, but this is where Pearson wanted to be, and he was very happy. He had a home, a son, and his Baby Doll.

As the years passed, the farm grew and five other children were born. Life was hard but Pearson and Mandy loved their children and were very happy.

Pearson and Mandy had been married for forty-five years when Pearson died on April 30, 1968 in Sylva, Jackson County, North Carolina, leaving Mandy to spend the next thirty five years without him. On December 23, 2003, Pearson was reunited with his Baby Doll when Mandy passed away at Mountain Trace Nursing Center in Webster, Jackson County, North Carolina.

A Mountain Tale of Love
by Jerry Owen

Each year when we have our Owen Family Reunion, we try to set a central theme which follows a time period in our family history. As a part of this, we do multi-media shows as well as perform live skits and dramas. In 2003 our theme was the Winds of War and our time period was the years just preceding the Civil war until around 1895. One of the family dramas we performed that year involved the love affair between my 2nd great-grandparents, William Jackson Owen, "Jackie" and Elizabeth Jane Owen, "Lizbeth". The entire script would be entirely too long for this venue, so I decided to tell the story and occasionally throw in some of the dialog from the skit.

Jackie and Lizbeth- A Mountain Love Story

Jackie and Lizbeth Owen were cousins. Jackie was the son of James "Jimmy" and Lizzie Owen, and Lizbeth was the daughter of Jesse and Juda Owen. In the years leading up to the Civil war, they both were young teenagers attending school in a one room school on Owen property known as the Owen School, along with several other mountain children. Jackie was about five years older than Lizbeth and for most of the years he had known her, he just considered her a pesky little girl cousin. Jackie was a tall, rugged, strong and handsome young man for his time, and was the apple of many a young mountain girl's eye. In fact, his father Jimmy had to make peace with more than one irate mountain father over his romantic and rambunctious son.

Sometime around 1859, Jackie suddenly began to see Lizbeth in a different light. In that year, Jackie had turned 18 and Lizbeth was now 13. Our drama begins with Jackie and Lizbeth at the little Owen Schoolhouse. On this particular day some older boys from up on Wolf Mountain had decided to pay a visit to the school to check out the blossoming young girls. They waited until recess time and just sort of slipped out of the woods. One of the boys was especially taken with Lizbeth.

This particular boy was well known as a bully and, as bullies are prone to do, he did not fight fair. Anytime anyone stood up to him he would pull his knife which he kept hidden in his boot. In the past this bluff had served him well. Jackie knew as well as anyone else that this could turn ugly, but he decided then and there that this had gone on long enough. One of the traits Jackie had inherited from his Owen ancestors was a sense of justice and, in his eyes, this situation needed a quick and decisive dose of mountain justice. Jackie walked straight up to the bully and told him in no uncertain terms to leave the girl alone and get on back to whatever hole he had crawled out of. The bully did not appreciate any of this and immediately pulled his knife on Jackie.

What happened next became a part of mountain lore to be talked about for years to come. In less time than it took to think about it, Jackie reached out his muscled long arm, grabbed the bully by the shirt, lifted him off the ground at least two feet and slapped him ten times back and forth so hard it made the boy's teeth rattle, caused him to drop his knife and wet his pants all at the same time. As soon as Jackie let him go, the bully and his friends made a hasty exit and never came back to the Owen School again.

Something changed in Lizbeth's heart on that day and she knew she would never be able to look at Jackie the same again. Jackie walked about a quarter mile with Lizbeth and her younger brother, Sam, that day just to be sure they were not followed by the bully and friends.

The following conversation was a part of our family skit dialog.

Lizbeth: Jackie, why did you do that for me today? You could have been hurt bad.

Jackie: I don't hold with bullies especially when they are messing with my family and even more so when it is you, Lizbeth.

Lizbeth: Why especially me Jackie? (looking questioningly into his steel grey eyes)

Jackie: I like you, Liz--I like you a lot-- I feel good when I am around you, that's all. (Jackie shrugs.)

Jackie was embarrassed by now and soon turned back towards his home, but something special had just passed between them, and he felt it all the way back up the mountain.

When we next encounter these two budding lovers, we find them at a large Owen family gathering in 1860. Jackie is now 19 and Lizbeth is all of 14. This gathering was called by the Patriarch of the Owen family, John W. Owen. John was well aware of the terrible war that was already looming over everyone's heads. Many of the mountain families, including the Owen family, were divided right down the middle as to where their loyalties lay. Some had already joined the Confederate army and a few had slipped over the mountains to Tennessee to join the Yankee army.

John was hoping that this large family gathering could some way hold the family together rather than have it ripped apart. John's home was about half way between Jimmy and Jesse's homes so both families had come prepared to spend the night. During the day on Saturday, most of the men smoked tobacco, talked about the war and occasionally shared a jug of fine whiskey. The women spent the day cooking and catching up on family news. It was during this time that Jackie and Lizbeth were able to slip away and spend some time together on the banks of the French Broad River. We pick up the family skit here.

Lizbeth: I heard that your family is moving to Georgia. Jackie, I can't bear for you leave me all alone in these mountains. I don't know exactly what it means, but I am never happy when I am not with you.

Jackie: I feel the same about you, Liz.

Lizbeth: But you have a lot of girls who like you. Why would you ever miss me?

Jackie: (Takes Lizbeth's hand and looks her in the eye) Liz, I have never said this to any girl. I don't know why, but I know I love you.

Lizbeth: (squeezes his hand hard, looks off into the distance and says with tears in her eyes) I love you, too!

Almost simultaneously they embrace and slowly move together. They have never kissed before and the emotion is so strong it almost feels like time has slowed down to a crawl as their lips meet. Jackie and Lizbeth share a long slow and tender kiss.

After the families have parted and Jackie and Lizbeth are back on their own mountains, the memory of that single slow kiss haunts both of them night and day. The only thing either one can think about is the fire that runs between them when they even slightly touch. Jackie decides that he has to have Lizbeth for his wife or life just won't be worth anything ever again. When he thinks of her laugh, her beautiful dark hair and blue eyes, he is overcome with the desire to have and to hold her. Jackie makes a decision that will change his life forever. He decides to talk with both his father, James, and his Uncle Jesse and tell them how he feels about Lizbeth.

This is the scene in the skit where he talks to his dad.

Jackie: Daddy, I am in love. I know Lizbeth is my cousin, but I love her as much as any man has ever loved a woman and I intend to make her my wife.

Jimmy: (looks at his son for the longest time and finally says) Jackie, I can see from the look on your face you are telling the truth about your feelings. (Shakes his head sadly) Lizbeth is so young and Jesse is a stubborn proud man. I know how he feels about that girl, and I don't believe he will ever allow her to marry you.

Jackie: I know this feeling I have is right and, if there is a God in heaven, He will help me with this. I just wanted you to know now before we leave this country; I will either be taking Lizbeth with me or I will not be going to Georgia with you.

Jimmy: Son, you do what you feel is right and be a man about it, and I will stand behind you all the way.

Next we find Jackie and Lizbeth talking with Jesse and Juda.

Jackie: Uncle Jesse, I love Lizbeth and I am asking you for her hand in marriage. (Lizbeth blushes, moves closer to Jackie and tells her dad she loves Jackie as well.)

Jesse: (Anger rising in his face) Jackie, I've always liked you and I know you are a true Owen, but there's no way on God's earth you will ever marry my daughter! (He stands and begins gesturing as he becomes more angry) My God, man, she is only 14 years old. She is just a baby and besides that I intend for her to marry someone besides her own cousin.

Jackie: (his own anger rising) Uncle Jesse, it is not unusual for cousins to marry here in the mountains and many girls that I know have married at 14.

Jesse: Many girls may marry this early but my Lizbeth is not going to be one of them. You have absolutely nothing to offer her and will only bring her a life of sorrow and an early grave.

Jackie: (Becomes very upset; Lizbeth is crying now and Jackie raises his voice at Jesse.) I don't care what you say, we love each other and there's nothing you can do about it.

Jesse: I tell you what, you young pup, you have exactly two minutes to get out of my house or I will blow your head off even if you are my nephew. Nobody comes to my house and talks to me like that.

Needless to say Jackie left that day with a sad heart and a dark brooding dislike for his uncle Jesse.

On the day James Owen finally began the arduous trip through the mountains moving his family lock, stock and barrel from their North Carolina home to the new home in the mountains of Georgia, this tale takes two different courses.

Family Oral History

According to stories passed down through the family, James and family, including Jackie, began the trip at night and came within a half mile of Jesse's home. The story continues that Jackie walked the remainder of the way to Jesse's crawling the last hundred feet or so on his belly. He then threw meat to the dogs to keep them quiet and Lizbeth, who knew he was coming, came out to meet him. They walked back to the wagon, climbed aboard and by early morning they were all many miles away. Jackie and Lizbeth were married and lived happily ever after.

Facts and Research Story

Jackie and Lizbeth's first child, Margaret M Owen, and their second child, William Sherman Owen, my great-grandfather, were both born in Transylvania County, NC, Margaret in 1862 and Sherman in 1864. It was not until 1866 that their third child, Jeremiah McClellan Owen, was born in Georgia. This seems to indicate that Jackie either stayed behind when the family moved, or that he went to Georgia and came back at a later time and got Lizbeth. More research will have to be done to figure out which way it happened. Either way, Jackie and Lizbeth were married and remained together until 1884 when she died giving birth to twins, Albert and Allice Owen

Little Owen Schoolhouse

Leaving the Mountains
by Jerry Owen

From 1892 until 1908, the William Sherman Owen family lived on the side of a mountain which straddled Towns County, GA and Clay County, NC. My grandfather, Jesse Luon Owen, was just a lad of nine years old in 1908 when the family decided to leave the mountains forever and move to Grayson County, Texas. The luring factor was the possibility of a better way of life raising cotton on a black-land farm. In the mountains, the family was farmers and stock raisers and, on occasions when the crops failed, had to resort to brewing and selling moonshine just to survive. Sarah was a strict fundamentalist Christian and did not approve of alcohol for any reason. This move represented an opportunity to keep her sons from following in the footsteps of their father, Sherman and their grandfather, Jackie Owen.

Lylish Eller and Julia Owen

In 1906, the Owen family was hit hard by a terrible tragedy. My grandfather's oldest sister, Julia, died in childbirth that year. Julia had married Lylish Eller against the family's wishes in 1902. The Owen family and the Eller family were never on very good terms and had from time to time feuded. Being the oldest child, all the other children looked up to her and missed her terribly when she married and moved away from the family. Lylish and Julia set up housekeeping on Eller property further up on Upper Bell Creek, a few miles from the Owen home. Lylish was a very serious and strict husband and life for Julia was not as happy in her new home as she had hoped. The family always enjoyed and looked forward to visits from Julia, but Lylish made sure these visits were few and far in between. In the dead of the cold hard winter of

1906 when snow covered the mountains, Julia went into labor and suffered many agonizing hours of pain before giving birth to stillborn twin daughters. Sadly she did not live but a few hours after giving birth. For many reasons the Owen family laid the blame for the loss of their dear sweet sister and daughter on Lylish and his family.

My grandfather remembered Julia's funeral and burial as long as he lived. He could never talk about her without getting a very sad look on his face and, on occasion, would even shed a tear when talking about his sister. Relating the scene at the grave was the most painful for him. He said the burial was in the early afternoon and, after everyone else had gone, all Julia's brothers and sisters and her parents, William Sherman and Sarah, just could not bear to leave her and were still there when the sun began to set. They all sang "Amazing Grace" over and over and, for the remainder of his life, that was his favorite song. It always took him back there to that day every time he heard it. On the day the family actually left the mountains for good Julia's grave was the last stop they made in Towns County. He would later say they all wanted to dig her up and take her to Texas with them, but of course they couldn't. The hardest part of leaving for all of them was leaving Julia behind.

It was right after Julia's death, while everyone was still dealing with this aching grief in their own way, that the decision was made to move to Texas. My grandfather often wondered if her death and the hard manner in which both Sherman and Sarah took her passing may have influenced them to leave the mountains for a better way of life and maybe to find away to heal.

After the decision to move was made, many things still had to be done to actually be able to close out their life in the mountains and begin the journey to the great state of Texas. It was early autumn in 1908 before the move finally took place. In the intervening time, the Owen mountain property was sold for $300. This was a considerable sum of money at that time. One important thing as far as Sarah was concerned was to make a last visit to her parent's home in Macon County, NC. In addition to wanting to see her parents again, she very much wanted her children to be able to spend time with their grandparents. She knew that, with moving so far away, it might be the last time any of them would have that opportunity. Time would prove this premonition to be true.

On the appointed day for this trip to Smithbridge, Macon County, NC to begin, a little hitch in plans arose. Sherman was a temperamental man and tended to become quite obstinate when he was upset. On the morning of the trip, he flat said he wasn't going, and it appeared that all the wagon loading and food preparation for the trip was all for naught. My grandfather remembered that everyone was very dejected, because they knew Sherman would not change his mind. Sarah, however, was bound and determined to see her parents one last time and told him in no uncertain terms that she and the kids were going to NC, whether he went along or not. He became belligerent and walked off through the woods, and Sarah and the kids crawled in the wagon and headed off down the road. They did not see Sherman again until they returned from NC.

This was a very hard and sometimes dangerous trip across the mountains at that time and not at all like the short day trip it is today. It took three days and nights of travel in that wagon just to get there. The mountains were scary at night and all kinds of wild animals could be heard screaming and growling near the camp. The most aggressive predators in those mountains of the great dark Nantahala forest were wolves and mountain panthers. My grandfather's three oldest brothers, Selly, Paul, and Marsen, all took turns staying awake during the night to make sure the fire of the camp did not burn out. They all felt that the fire was all that kept the wolves at bay. When telling this story, my grandfather had a way of scaring the "bejeebers" out of us grandchildren when talking about the unearthly screams of the panthers and the eerie howling of the wolves. For some reason it seemed he always liked to tell this story at night just before everyone went to bed.

Early the next morning, after a hearty campfire breakfast, the wagon would roll again. After the three day journey, everyone was overjoyed to see their grandparents and spent several happy days visiting with them before making the long trip back through the mountains and forests.

On one of these days arrangements were made to get a local photographer from Franklin to come out and make a family portrait. This was the very last time Sarah saw her parents and the last time most of the children saw them, making this a very special portrait for the family.

On April 24, 1908 Sarah gave birth to twins, Maud Este Owen and Aud Veste Owen. Just a few months later the journey to Texas was underway and the legend of the Buttermilk Trail was born. Look for that story in another section of this book!

Thomas Rhodes Family

A Visit to Wolf Mountain
by Karen Medlock Pettit

This is a personal story of an experience which took place when I was a little girl. I believe I was about nine, ten at the most, but I remember the day as if it happened yesterday.

Ruth Owen Galloway, wife of James Fred Galloway, was my dad's aunt, the sister of his mother, Ella Owen Medlock. Grandmother Ella died when my dad was a small boy, but he remembered her amazingly well and many times spoke of her. He kept in touch with his Aunt Ruth over the years, and one day, it was decided among the grown-ups (Dad and Mother, my Aunt Elsie Medlock Alexander and Uncle

Ralph, her husband), that our families would make a trip together to Wolf Mountain to visit their Aunt Ruth and her family.

I imagine the plans for that visit were discussed and approved by Aunt Ruth; in other words, a trip up to Wolf Mountain from down in Pickens County wasn't just something that was decided upon on the spur of the moment. I can remember fording a shallow creek in the cars to get to where the Galloways lived, and I remember I thought that was quite something in itself! We did get to the other side safely, drove up a road, of sorts, and suddenly came to a partial clearing where suddenly there appeared a house. I can remember the steps that led up to the porch. As a child being taken on this trip by my parents and aunt and uncle (along with their children), I had no idea where we were or why we were there.

Now, my cousins who were along for that trip took after their daddy's side of the family, meaning that they had dark hair and eyes, with the exception of my cousin Frank whose coloring was a bit lighter, light brown hair and lighter colored eyes, but still, all in all, much different from me.....I was blonde! The only one in the whole group, and there were times I wondered if I really "belonged" to that crowd! Then suddenly, to my amazement, out of the door of the house came a woman with blonde hair, and then from what seemed to be every direction imaginable, children...blonde-haired children!! It didn't take me too long to figure that somehow I had to be connected to these people!! I can remember actually being totally amazed and thrilled at the site of the strangers (to me, at least) who looked like I should be living with them instead of my own family!!

Most of the children were boys, and they ran and rough and tumbled all over the place as I sat on the front porch in total awe. I saw them "rassle" on the ground. One fell over a tree stump but got up laughing; I thought he probably had died the minute he fell over that big tree stump with pieces jutting out like spears!

The day wore on and we became a little friendlier to each other, more comfortable I guess you could say, and I got to where I could remember some of their names. Two of the boys looked to be about my own age. They disappeared for a while and then came back with a bucket of some kind. One of them came over to me with the bucket and asked me if I wanted some "chinkipins". Well, I said "no", because I didn't know what chinquapins were or what to do with them. But the boys were polite and I realized later that they were being nice and offering me some of the nuts they had gathered.

One of Aunt Ruth's daughters had been peeking through the screen door for what seemed a long time, and finally someone told her to come on out and meet us, that we were "kin people", so she came and sat on the top step. My daddy, trying to make friendly conversation with her, made a comment that she was a real pretty girl and he bet there were some nice boys who came calling. It just embarrassed her to death, and she got up, ran inside the house, and hid behind the door for a long time until her daddy explained that my daddy was saying something nice about her and told her to come on back outside and quit being "ornery" because "he didn't mean no harm". My daddy felt bad for embarrassing her and he told her he was sorry, that he meant what he said in a real good way. I can remember her nodding her head and looking at him and sorta smiling, like maybe he was an okay person after all.

The day began waning, and Aunt Ruth had us all come inside and there was what looked like an absolute feast on a long table, all set up for us. I can't remember everything the meal consisted of, but I do remember a pitcher of milk, fresh picked blackberries, and hot biscuits that tasted like heaven to me that day! It finally came time for us to leave, and everybody gathered around and said goodbyes before we started back down the mountain. I remember we were invited to come back again and Aunt Ruth and Uncle Fred saying it was nice having us for company, and the kids all said it was a pleasure making acquaintance with us. The two younger boys brought me a little brown paper sack half-filled with "chinkipins" for me to take home with me.

It has been many years since that visit, but it has remained vivid in my memory. As I grew older, I came to appreciate and understand it more and more, and in my adulthood, I have always been very thankful I had the opportunity that day to visit my kin on Wolf Mountain. I have often wondered over the years if my "cuzzins" remembered us as vividly as I do them.

The Cherry Tree Incident
by Winnie Kropelnicki

All of these mountains surrounding my home here on my Great-Grandfather John B. Owen's home place were originally Owen family property. Much of it is still in the family. John's property went all the way up the side of the mountains that lead to Lake Toxaway. He shared a common boundary line with land owned by his brother, Jesse Owen. Jesse lived on mountain property that is about half way between Lake Toxaway and my home today. It was sometimes difficult to tell exactly where the line lay, and in most cases, it did not matter that much to any of the brothers. As each new generation of the family would reach the age of having a family of their own, they would usually be given or sold a small piece of the original property to farm and to make a home. Sometimes this led to small disputes but they were usually easy to work out. This incident was the result of this sort of next-generation land usage.

My grandfather, Alfred Henry Owen, had assumed ownership of the John B. Owen property and Jesse Owen's son, Elijah Dillard Owen, was living on the original Jesse Owen home place. Alfred gave one of his sons, John Harrison Owen, some land that connected with the land that belonged to Elijah Dillard Owen. We all just refer to him as Uncle John. In the mountains at that time, fruit trees were very important and provided both a food source and a way to make money for families. Uncle John set out a nice orchard of trees. From what I can remember I think my dad said they were cherry trees. Apples and cherries were some of the most popular and healthy trees that grew in these mountains at that time. Uncle John was very proud of his trees, especially one really nice healthy cherry tree. Uncle John would go and spend time working with them each day after he had finished all his other work. Elijah Dillard caught him one day and pointed out to Uncle John that his orchard was slightly over the line and on his property. Uncle John was a little strong willed himself and told Elijah that, regardless, they were his trees and that was the end of that. After a few more such interchanges between these two strong-willed and resolute Owen men, no good solution had been arrived at. One day when Uncle John went to check on his cherry trees he was horrified to see that several had been chopped or sawed down, including his favorite tree which had obviously been sawed down. To say that Uncle John was incensed would be an understatement. He was livid but did not know exactly what to do or who to blame.

One of the strict codes in the mountains was to show honor to your elders, so he did not want to immediately blame his uncle Elijah, and he couldn't be sure that it was Elijah who did this terrible thing. The only natural thing to do was to consult his father, Alfred Henry. Alfred, along with Pete Owen, accompanied Uncle John to the destroyed orchard. Pete was a man of few words but everyone knew that when he did speak it was best to pay attention. Alfred and Pete stood and looked at the chopped trees for several minutes without saying a word. Then Pete looked Uncle John directly in the eye and said in a dead serious voice. "Well, John, I don't know who did this, but I can say it was a left handed sawyer."

This was the end of the Cherry Tree Incident but many family stories indicate that Elijah Dillard Owen may have been left handed.

Memories of a Granny

by Linda Owen Anders

The light from the window fell on her white hair and created a halo that surrounded her head. A look of love softened the wrinkles of nine decades as she looked down at the baby in her arms. Thoughts and memories of long ago rose within her.

Her life had been devoted to babies--ten of her own--including her baby boy who had died. She had been called many times, day and night, to help "catch" a baby and always kept her "kit" ready to go. Over the years had come many grandchildren and now great-grandchildren like the little one she was holding.

Time had taught her to be content with simple things. Her plain dress with the pin on the front. Hair pulled back in a knot at the back of her neck. The old two-story house with red siding, a big front porch and tall fir tree in the front yard. Crocheted pieces on the arms of the overstuffed sofa and chairs. Sitting on the front porch in warm weather watching the cars come and go along the highway--she could remember the first car she had ever seen! Or, in cold weather, sitting on her enclosed porch in the back of the house, crocheting and knitting. Even now, she was still caring for her babies, for she had just finished knitting a cap for her son, in his sixties but still her little boy. And this baby, so tiny against her large frame, was wearing little yellow booties she had knit.

She was content with life but not content to let life pass her by unnoticed. She knew all the local happenings and enjoyed talking about them with her many visitors. Knowing where her grandchildren had moved and what was happening in their lives, she was the link that held her large family together. Yet, she let the young people live their own lives and make their own decisions. She had never meddled in other people's affairs. When she was young, she had seen women wear bustles as "big as peck buckets". Of course, she had never worn such a contraption! Women wearing pants? Well, she still preferred dresses that reached nearly to her ankles, but what they wore was their own business.

Her younger brother, only in his eighties, had visited the other day. He had begun to condemn the current generation, quoting from the Bible, when she stopped him abruptly. "Don't start telling me what the Bible says! I've read my Bible more times than you," she said, "even if you are a preacher." The years had taught her how to apply its teaching to her life, too.

She had not always been so peace-loving. "I was wild as a girl," she told her granddaughter, not using the word as it would be used today but meaning "wild and untamed like the mountains where I grew up." She had been close to all the other living, growing things. She had known where to find the herbs and roots which she could dry. She had walked miles across the mountains to sell them and buy ribbons for her bonnet and for her sisters, too.

Memories bound her to these mountains where her family had lived for many years. She was born Florence Caledonia Hall, on Scotts Creek, Jackson County, NC, and was the oldest child of William Elbert and Altha Owen Hall. Her great-great-great-great-grandfather Joshua Hall, a Baptist minister, had pioneered nearby Macon County and was buried there with his wife, Sarah. Her grandparents and great-grandparents were buried at the Scotts Creek cemetery, as was her little brother who had only lived three months.

She had first attended school in Jackson County where the only textbook was the old blue-back speller. School lasted six weeks. Her family then moved to the higher mountains of Transylvania County, NC, seeking refuge from "milk sickness", a mysterious illness which did not affect the cows but was sometimes fatal to humans. There she had finished her education, attending school from July to November each year, with two weeks off to take in fodder and gather the crops. She had only to take an exam to be a teacher herself. College degrees

Florence and Rufus Owen with daughter Grace

were not required for teachers then.

Tall and slender, with an 18-inch waist, all the boys had admired her. "I wouldn't let nary one hold my hand or walk me home after church," she said. Then Rufus William Owen came along, with his wit and charm and his smiling face, and she could not resist him. She gave up her plans to be a teacher and became his wife.

She was 18 years old when they were married at his father's home. They stayed with his family until they could get a place of their own, as most young people did in those days. Only a week after they were married, she had been stricken with typhoid fever. For 21 days, she hadn't known anything. Rufus had stayed by her side and his family helped to nurse her. After she recovered, she was still so weak that she could not walk to the neighbors without taking a piece of bread and stopping to eat. Then someone suggested she try chewing tobacco; she tried it--and it became a lifelong habit. "Course I don't use it strong," she explained.

Times had been tough, but people had plenty to eat if they were willing to work hard and raise it themselves. Food had occupied much of her time, planting, gathering, storing, and cooking it. Her family had raised buckwheat. After harvesting, they would shovel out a hole in the ground, line it with wagon sheets, put the buckwheat into the middle and beat it with hickory poles. When the wind blew, they would hold the sheets up by the corner and let the wind blow the husks away. After it was cleaned in this way, the buckwheat was taken to the mill to be ground.

Bread was baked in the fireplace by heaping coals over a covered iron pot. On special occasions, they would make "light bread" which had to be left to rise in the sun several days. They grew peaches and apples and dried them; also, they smoked apples with sulfur to keep them fresh. They preserved barrels of pickled beans and sauerkraut. She remembered long tables of food, at home as a child, as her own children grew up, and at family celebrations and reunions through the years. She still made sure that no one left her house hungry and always kept homemade pound cake to offer her visitors.

Her first child was born shortly after their first anniversary and the babies continued to come every two to three years for the next twenty years. Thinking back, the years seemed to have gone by quickly. Her marriage with "Little Ruf", as he was called, had been a happy one. "We never had a short word with one another and I guess we was as happy a couple as ever lived," she reminisced. They had built this house together over 60 years ago. "When we moved here, women laughed at me because I rode horses. The women here didn't ride horses; they had buggies. I loved to ride and could ride any horse, side-saddle, of course. Had a special riding outfit." But she soon had a buggy of her own, too, which she drove on Sunday, with all the children, her own and the neighbors, piled on it, arms and legs sticking out, going for a fast ride.

She had seen many changes in her life. Once she caught the train to her brother's, who was sick, and sat up all night with him. As she was getting ready to leave the next morning to catch the train home, the doctor invited her to ride with him in his new automobile, the first one in the county. The road was very rough and the car went so fast she had to "hang on for dear life." Another change was when Rufus bought a crank-up Victrola. All the neighbors gathered at night to listen to it. The children finished their chores quickly for some time!

The clothes were boiled in a big black pot, and she beat them with a battling stick--she kept another stick, too, which she used to keep the children in line! If it wasn't handy, she used whatever was nearby. Rufus didn't have the heart to discipline the children--he had vivid memories of his own childhood and how he had suffered from abuse--so it was left to her, and six rowdy boys took a lot of discipline!

She made all their clothes, even men's pants and underwear, and not from store-bought cloth either. She would gather barks, flowers and roots to dye the cloth, which she wove from homespun thread. She added little stones to the dye to set the colors. In later years, she dyed flour sacks and made flowers to decorate her quilts, some of which took prizes at the county fair.

When they first built their house, it was only one story, but later they added bedrooms upstairs. The only source of heat was the fireplace. At night, the children would warm by it and then run upstairs and jump in bed. They slept on straw mattresses--"ticks", which were filled each year with new straw and fluffed up high. She chuckled as she remembered how she had refilled them and moved the furniture around one year. That night one of her sons, after getting warm by the fire, had run and jumped onto the bureau instead of the bed!

There were many good memories, but some were not good. A sadness came over her as she thought of her mother who had died before her second baby was born. Also, she remembered living through two world wars, with four sons and a son-in-law in the last one. But her faith had carried her through it all.

Sometimes it had taken her time to adjust--like the time her son, 29-years old, had come home with his 16-year old wife, a girl she had never met before. She didn't say a word--just got up and packed his clothes. Rufus talked a lot trying to cover up for her; he had felt sorry for the "little thing." Later, she literally got sick about acting that way and sent word to them to come see her. She gave them some quilts and other things to help start their home.

But the hardest time had come when she lost her love, Rufus, after 68 years of marriage. She bent over him as he lay in the coffin and kissed him. "I'll be with you soon," she said. Now she was passing the years away quietly, remembering, but also living day by day. Her own granny had lived to be 93 years old. She wondered, could she pass that mark?

The years have passed. The baby who had been nestled in Granny's arms is now a grown woman and expecting a baby of her own, but she has memories, too. As a little girl she had said to her Mommy, "I love her so much. I wish Granny didn't have to die." Mommy replied, "I know, dear, I miss her, too. But she lived 94 good years..."

Written as a tribute to my Granny, Florence Hall Owen, born 1885, died 1979.

METAL MONSTER
by Mary Ellen Yelton

My mother, Gladys Hoyle, and her family lived at Balsam. They were a poor family and stayed to themselves, hardly ever seeing anyone but family. One day Gladys and her sisters, Lou Ellen and Nelia, were outside in the logging road playing. All of a sudden, they heard the loudest, scariest noise they had ever heard, and it was coming their way! Gladys looked up to see this big ol' metal monster moving up the road right towards them. Not knowing what it was, she grabbed Lou Ellen's hand and raced for the house and hid them both under the bed. She was terrified. She could laugh about it later. Gladys had just seen her first CAR!!!!!!

OLLIE'S SEWING MACHINE
by Mary Ellen Yelton

Ollie and Gill Hoyle were my maternal grandparents. They mostly lived in Andrews, N.C. or Balsam, N.C. Gill must have been full of wanderlust because he moved his family from Andrews to Balsam, and even to Clover, S.C. several times. This one particular time, they lived in Clover, and he got to hankering to go back to Jackson County and settle at Scott's Creek. He had no money. The only way they could move back to the mountains was to sell something. He slipped around and sold my grandmother's prized sewing machine! When he told my grandmother, she cried for days.

I don't know if she ever got over that. Imagine having a large family, mostly girls, husband has no regular job, and your sewing machine is sold to move YET again!! The last time they moved, they moved to Gastonia, N.C. where they both died.

BONEY'S DEFEAT
by Shawna Hall

In the Little Canada section of Jackson County, N.C. there is a 400-foot sheer rock cliff just off Highway 281 called Bonas Defeat. When my great-great-great-grandfather, Andrew Jackson "Andy" Wood, moved to this area about 1840, there was nothing there but magnificent untouched wilderness and plentiful wild game. Andrew Jackson Wood was born in 1816, shortly after Andrew Jackson defeated the British at New Orleans, and was named in honor of him.

According to my grandmother, Andy Wood was a hunter of some fame and had a pack of dogs that he ran deer with. His favorite hunting dog was called Boney, so named because of his body build. Andy loved that dog beyond measure. One day Andy and Boney were running a deer near this cliff. Andy was lagging behind Boney, following his barks and bays, when all of a sudden there was silence. When Andy got to the edge of the cliff, he looked down to the bottom of the gorge and there lay the deer and Boney side-by-side, both dead. The deer had gone right over that cliff and Boney had either followed him or been unable to stop at the precipice.

Andy managed to hike down to the bottom of the cliff and sat crying beside his dog for some time. After a while he picked up Boney's broken body and carried him home. For months afterward, Andy told of his beloved dog's fate to family, friends and neighbors, always ending the story with "That cliff was Boney's defeat". So of course residents of the area began calling the cliff Boney's Defeat. Over the years the name somehow changed to Bonas Defeat, but to this day it remains a living memorial to Andy Jackson Wood's beloved hunting dog.

SAREE CRACK
by Jerry Owen

My great-grandmother, Sarah Elizabeth Rhodes Owen, was a very disciplined and organized person. I think it may have been the German blood coming out in her. From what I can find out there is a German Rhodes family, originally spelled Rodt-- and an English Rhodes family. I think my Rhodes are German but I can't be sure. They are all fairly good-looking people, handsome men and beautiful women, but very regimented and stern.

My great-grandmother, also a very beautiful woman, was the one who originated the Saree Crack that has passed down through our family. The way it worked was that when you were at the table eating, if you were one of the children, you didn't talk and mess around or suddenly you would be cracked in the head with a large wooden spoon. My granddad said you could see it coming, moving up and down and gaining momentum as it went. Everyone in our family incorporated the Saree Crack in our table manners including me. My son Tony was the one who finally broke the old tradition.

We were sitting at the table at Denny's restaurant when he was just about three years old. He was being a real mess and throwing food and making faces, etc., so I pulled out the trusty old Saree Crack maneuver. Immediately after I cracked him (easily of course), he grabbed the spoon and began hitting himself in the head as hard as he could. It scared us so bad I never used the Saree Crack again. I don't know if any one else in our family still uses it or not. It's sad to see old customs go but I think it was time for this one to become history.

Sarah was a big influence on my granddad, and one of the rules she instituted that he was fanatical about was "A place for everything and everything in its place." If I had to guess I would say there is definitely German influence there. My friend Richard Limbock who is German, says his mother used many of these same strict rules. My mother was Irish, Murphy, and she was totally opposite. With her, eating as a family was actually fun. We always hated it when the Old Man made it home for dinner because all the fun stopped. You see of course he was a second generation descendant of the Queen of the Saree Crack, Sarah Elizabeth Rhodes Owen.

Sarah Elizabeth Rhodes Owen

Memories of my Nanny
Bessie Lee Gravley Anders, 1927 - 1997
by Heather Hogsed

I remember her hands were always soft; she used to use this lotion all the time...I used to put my little hands in hers to compare them.

She always used to make us kids little sleeping spots on the floor, almost like an Army corps, line us up one by one...and we would lay there while she watched Highway to Heaven, and curled her hair every night, one piece at a time.

Nanny loved to dance. I've never seen anything else like it. She would Buck dance, clog, and twist here and twist there, all bunched together in one...she could move...

She had that deep voice...and when she'd yell your name...it was magnificent...a two part tone...and she had that dog, "Honey" that used to smile at you...she was raggedy and beautiful...I remember Nanny would have us take left-over food outside and dump it beside the tree for the dogs...yes, a bunch of dogs would tend to stop by.

I remember her taking us mining a couple of times. She loved that! Where you put the dirt inside the little basket thing and water would flow to reveal the rocks. I probably never got anything valuable, but Nanny always said "Ooh...that's a pretty one" like I had found gold.

In Nanny there was gold, a heart full of it. She always had a sparkle in her eye. When we moved to our new house in Germany, Nanny came along with us. I remember Nanny and I used to sit outside on the balcony and play Rummy. Nanny loved to play Rummy!

And she got me addicted to it! We would sit out on our balcony for hours, playing Rummy and talking.

We used to always take walks in Germany as well. We'd walk around town, picking blackberries, looking at everything...looking at everybody...there was this one older Frenchman who used to ride his bicycle up and down the street and he would wave at us, mainly Nanny. Nanny used to talk like she was gonna call back home and tell them that a Frenchman took her for a ride on his bicycle...it was the funniest thing.

Ooh, I loved her blackberry cobbler, it was absolutely spectacular. Nanny was always eating Butterfingers and all those little peanut candies.

When I think of Nanny I think of God. She would talk to me forever about Him… she was really a main influence in my life as far as religion goes…she would recite these beautiful poems off the top of her head, and tell me she wrote them…and she did. She wrote the prettiest poems ever.

The day before she passed away, I spoke to her on the phone. I told her that I loved her…asked her how she was doing…she told me "The angels are coming to get me" and that is something that I will never forget…anytime I see an angel statue or an angel painting I always think of her, because in my heart, she will always be an angel.

Bessie Lee Gravley Anders

Life Story of Perry Fields Gravley
by Steve Powell

On June 24th, 1893, Perry Fields Gravley, the child of Richard and Elizabeth Gilstrap Gravley, was born in a small house near the Oolenoy River in upper Pickens County, South Carolina.

Perry's father, Richard, ran a small farm and grist mill in the Holly Springs section of Pickens County. He loved working his farm and taught his children to love the land and values of knowing how to use it.

Perry's mother, Elizabeth, a very robust energetic woman, helped Richard run the mill and also raised their very large family. They had 17 children; twelve of these reached adulthood. She was also considered the local doctor by the people who lived around there. She didn't have very much formal education but she taught herself, through practical experience and attending a few classes, to learn about medicine. She often would go to the houses of her neighbors and help with the sick or deliver babies or whatever was necessary.

Perry attended Holly Springs School where he attained a seventh grade education, which was above average schooling for that particular time and place. When he wasn't going to school, Perry worked on the farm and helped run the mill along with his brothers.

Perry always had a very good sense of humor and was usually slow to anger. As a result of this, he often caught the brunt of practical jokes played by his brothers. Like the time he was riding a mule and his brothers got beside it and ran it toward a tree, making Perry fall off. He took all their jokes in stride and would eventually somehow get even with them.

One of the main things that Richard raised on his farm was hogs. It was the custom back then for each family to mark their hogs a certain way and then turn them loose. Nobody would ever kill another man's hog if it had his mark on it. Once a year all the Gravley boys would have to go into the mountains to round the hogs up for butchering, often staying as much as a week at a time. Perry hated this particular chore, especially having to locate the hogs and bring them back to camp. So he was always assigned the job of staying behind at the wagon and being the cook. Once, to spite everybody, he cooked hog liver everyday for a week and everyone got sick.

When Perry was nineteen, he left Pickens and moved to Montana with his sister. While there, he stayed with a man named Mr. Fritters and helped him run a dairy. In the winter one of his jobs was to cut chunks of ice out of the river and store them in the ice house for use during the summer. One time, while returning from the river, the wagon hit a bump and threw Perry off. His hand got caught up in under the wheel crushing his thumb. The nearest hospital was thirty miles away and by the time he got there blood poisoning was already setting in. The doctor had to amputate his thumb in order to save his hand and probably his life.

Perry Fields Gravley (seated) with his brothers Benson and Ed

Perry stayed in Montana and worked for Mr. Fritters for four years. He returned to Pickens in 1916 and worked on the farm with his brothers.

After the war broke out in 1917, Perry felt it was his duty to enlist. He traveled to Greenville, South Carolina, to the induction center to offer his services. He was told he would never be able to get into the Army because of his thumb. So, disappointed, he returned home thinking he would have to wait out the war on the farm. Two months after he tried to enlist he received his draft notice. He was assigned to the 30th Infantry Division, nicknamed the Old Hickory Division, under the command of Captain Robert Cherry, who was later to become governor of North Carolina.

After a brief basic training in the summer of 1917, he was shipped to France. He was moved all over the country but mostly stayed in the northeastern part around Belgium. In spite of the war, Perry grew to love France and its people, naming his oldest daughter after one of its towns.

While he was in the war, he had a couple of pretty close calls. Once he was in a trench along with five other men when a mortar landed close by killing everyone but him. Perry was lucky he came out without a scratch in this incident. Another time, just before the raid on the Hindenburg line, Perry was caught in a gas attack by the Germans. As a result of this, he spent the remainder of the war in the hospital and didn't get to go with the rest of his troop into Germany at the war's end. He was released from the Army after the armistice, returning home secure in the knowledge that in some small way he had helped obtain peace.

About a year after he returned from the Army, Perry married Emma Cantrell, also a native of Pickens. Perry had known Emma for several years and had courted her while he was in the Army. Perry and Emma set up housekeeping in a small house across the road from Price's store in the Holly Springs section of Pickens. A year after they were married, a daughter whom they named Gladys Marcella was born to them.

A couple of years after they were married, tragedy suddenly struck the entire family. Perry's sister and brother-in-law, who lived down below the town of Pickens, contacted typhoid fever after drinking from a contaminated spring near their house. Naturally other members of the family at one time or another got sick.

Emma and Perry would often go to the house where a member of the family was sick, bringing food and helping out wherever they could. But Emma would always stay outside; she never went into the house where someone was sick, because she was afraid of contacting the disease herself. But unfortunately it was to no avail, a year after his sister first got sick, Perry and Emma came down with the fever. The doctor, who was overworked because of the epidemic, did all he could. An old black lady named Tina Webb, who lived around in that area and who often went to help nurse the sick and stayed with them, trying to nurse them both back to health. But in spite of everything Emma died. And Perry, who usually weighed around 160-165, lost down to 95 pounds and was so weak during Emma's funeral he had to be practically carried in and out of the church. In all, the typhoid epidemic took quite a toll on the Gravley family; Perry lost not only his wife but also two of his sisters, Dora and the youngest, Ellie, who was still living at home.

Less than a year after Emma died, Perry married Ella Polly Smith, also a native of Pickens County, who he had met through her father, an acquaintance of his. Ella was a very kind and gentle woman, who was a strong and steady influence on Perry and on the family they would eventually raise. After they were married, Ella immediately set up housekeeping and tended to the raising, and the caring of his baby daughter, Gladys.

Not long after they were married, Perry and his father-in-law started a business venture, which at the time was pretty prosperous, but was also dangerous and illegal. They set up a moonshine still, and made pretty good money at it for a while, until the federal men found it and cut it up. Perry managed to slip out without them catching him, but this was too close a call. Never again did he attempt to run a moonshine still. He returned to farming and running Price's store across from their house.

In February of the year 1924, Perry and Ella had another daughter whom they named Pauline Dalice. As his family grew, Perry's responsibilities also grew. Perry and Ella continued to run the store, but Perry also went to work at one of the local sawmills to help boost the family budget. Then in 1927 still another daughter, Bessie Lee, was born. After three daughters they decided to call it quits and they never had any more children.

In 1928, Perry bought a 65-acre tract of land, known as the Hines Place. It was located just across the state line in North Carolina, not far from the town on Rosman. Before moving his family, Perry hauled lumber across the mountain from South Carolina and built the house.

It included three big bedrooms, a big kitchen with a dining area, and a living room with fireplace. When the house was completed, he brought his family up from South Carolina and settled in.

In North Carolina, Perry ran a fairly big farm, in which he had a large number of hogs, several head of cattle, chickens, goats, and geese. The Mitch Aiken family lived on Perry's property and helped him run the farm.

Perry also ran a pretty profitable logging business. He owned his own truck and would haul cordwood off the mountain, selling it to Gloucester Lumber Company. The reason it was so profitable was because he wasn't afraid to take his truck anywhere, often taking his truck down steep mountain roads in order to get the best logs.

During the depression, Perry's skill as a farmer, along with his logging job, really paid off. While thousands of people during that time went hungry, Perry's family never wanted for food. One frequent visitor to his house once commented that "at Perry's house it always looked like Thanksgiving."

In politics Perry was always a strong Democrat; he thought Franklin D. Roosevelt was one of the greatest men who ever lived. While he never ran for any office himself, he actively supported local candidates and served as judge for his precinct for years.

In the late thirties, Perry moved off the mountain, selling his farm and buying a 26-acre tract of land, which was closer to school where his daughters went.

In 1944 Perry's wife Ella, who had been in failing health for several years, died. Perry and Ella had been married for over 20 years, and in that time they had become completely devoted to each other. Ella's death was a tremendous jolt for Perry, one that would take a long time for him to get over.

Soon after this, Perry went to work for the tannery in Brevard. He also did rockwork for a man named Mr. Jaffee, a wealthy person who had moved from up north to settle in the Middle Fork Community. Perry laid his driveway in rock and also the wall that goes up beside the drive. Later he was to do all the rockwork at Birdrock Falls.

In 1949, Perry married Charlotte Chapman, a widow with grown children of her own. Perry and Charlotte lived quite contentedly with each other until Perry's death. Charlotte was to outlive him by about two months.

Perry Fields Gravley will probably never go down in the history books as a great man, but he will always be remembered in the hearts of the people who knew and loved him.

CHAPTER 6
THE OWEN HYMN

"In God's wilderness lies the hope of the world – the great fresh, unblighted, unredeemed wilderness. The galling harness of civilization drops off, and the wounds heal ere we are aware."
-John Muir 1838-1914
Naturalist, writer, conservationist,
and founder of the Sierra Club.

Hymn of Owen Family

submitted by Jerry Owen

This was a Family Hymn sung at many of the old Owen family reunions in the mountains. It was originally shared with us by Cuzzin Bob Benton from his family files.

The Famous and Historic Hymn of the Owen Family
Sung to the tune of the "Battle Hymn of the Republic"

> There's something strong and mighty in a good old family name,
> And the name of Owen shineth high upon the scroll of fame,
> For nearly all the Owens have preserved a lofty aim;
> The clan goes marching on.
>
> Chorus
>
> Glory to the name of Owen
> Glory to the name of Owen
> Glory to the name of Owen
> The clan goes marching on
>
> The house of Owen cherishes traditions of the past. With the worlds great moments they have all their fortunes cast,
> And when they pledge their loyalty they're loyal to the last,
> The clan goes marching on.
>
> Repeat Chorus
>
> The Owen tribe is virile as their fathers were of old,
> Each century their numbers have increased a hundred fold,
> With all the world's best families the Owens are pure gold
> The clan goes marching on
>
> Repeat Chorus.

The Owen Hymn

Owen sons are always loyal, Owen daughters true and sweet,
More noble sires and daughters you may never hope to meet,
The stories of their lives and deeds with pleasure repeat,
The clan goes marching on.

Repeat Chorus

We have our Dukes and peasants, common folk and bluebloods too,
They greet each other gladly with a "Cousin Howdy Do",
This goes with all the Owens and goes with me and you,
The clan goes marching on.

Repeat Chorus

The Owens are all loyal to the good old U.S.A.
They love the flag of freedom and will follow it for aye,
The Owens do their duty and they never run away,
The clan goes marching on.

Repeat Chorus

To every corner of our land we sound the bugle call
A hundred thousand Owens hear and answer one and all,
You can hear their cohorts tramping like Niagara's water fall,
The clan goes marching on.

Repeat Chorus

If you claim the blood of Owen join the chorus of the clan,
In our records and reunions do the very best you can,
The name to highest honors, boost it every way you can,
The clan goes marching on.

Repeat Chorus

--Author unknown

INDEX

A

A. J. Chappel 48
Aaron Styles 33
Abraham Glazener 106
Aiken
  Mitch 138
Akron 87
Alabama
  Mobile 62
Albert Owen 115
Alexander
  Elsie Medlock 119
  Ralph 120
Alfred Henry Owen 58, 122
Allice Owen 115
almanac 98
Altar
  The 41
Altha Owen Hall 124
Amanda
  Garner Henderson 54, 55
  Queens 108
Amazing Grace 117
ancestry
  Dutch 52
Anders
  Bessie Lee Gravley 40, 41, 42, 132
  Linda 50, 52
  Linda Owen 107, 123
Andrews, North Carolina 129
Andrew
  Jackson "Andy" Wood 129
  Jackson Owen 47, 92
Apples
  Poisoned 27
Appomattox 50
April Montgomery 30, 63, 88, 91
Army 61
  carbine 59
  Confederate 53, 54, 58, 59, 62, 64
  Continental 105
  Federal 74
  Union 47
Arthur Tillman Owen 107
Ary 99
Ary
  Jane Lynch 106
  Stewart Price 106
Asheville 65, 66, 67
astrological signs 98
Atlanta
  Battle of 62
Aud Veste Owen 119
Aunt Fredna 91
Avery
  Uncle 25

B

Bailey
  Mrs. 67
Balsam, North Carolina 27, 129
Balsam Grove, North Carolina 87, 110
Bannister Lynch 106
battalion
  Folk's 66
Battle of
  Camden 105
  Guilford Courthouse 105
  Haw River 105
Baxter
  John, Col. 73
beans
  snapped 92
  burned 89
Beasley
  Esther 106
Beavers
  Tammy 56
Belgium 136
Benjamin James "Jim" Wilson 50, 52
Benton
  Bob 142
Beryl Morgan 110

145

Bessie Lee Gravley Anders 40, 41, 42, 132
Big
  Indian Creek 60
  Willow Creek 64
Birdrock Falls 138
Birdseye Food Company 87
Bitters
  Spring 84
blackberry
  cobbler 133
  picking 91
blizzard 38
Bob Benton 142
Bonas Defeat 129
Boney 130
Bonham, Texas 81
Bowen
  Reverend 109
Bracken
  Phoebe Serena 50
Brevard 138
British 129
buckwheat 126
Burgess
  Carolyn McCall 108
  Cynthia 108
burned
  beans 89
Burning Bush
  the, 31
Bush
  Burning, The 31
Butterfingers 133
buttermilk 92
Buttermilk Trail 90, 119

C

cake
  stack 89
California 87
Camden
  Battle of 105
Camp Douglas
  Illinois 48
  Letter 48

Cantrell
  Emma 136
Captain Robert Cherry 136
Caroline
  Margaret 35
  Owen Glazener 35
Carolyn McCall Burgess 108
cat-o-nine tails 23
Catherine Gage Wedge 19, 60, 100
Catheryne Faison Hufham Wynne 19
Cathey's Creek
  Baptist Church
    Cemetery 50
  Transylvania County, North Carolina 54
cauls 97, 100
Cedro Wooly, Washington 26
Celtic 98
cemeteries 18
Cemetery 36
  Scotts Creek 124
  Cathey's Creek Baptist Church 50
Chapman
  Charlotte 138
Charles Lay 105
Charlotte Chapman 138
Cherokee 28, 32, 99, 100
  beliefs
    race of little people 23
    respect to the old 25
  full-blooded 31
  haunted by the, 20
  heritage 31
  Hollow 33, 34
  Indians 39
  martyr
    Tsali 31
  removal 23
  trails 83
Cherry
  Robert, Captain 136
  Tree Incident 123
chinkipins 121
Chucky River 69
Civil War 52, 63, 81
  deserters 56
  Experience 50

in the Mountains 45
Mountain Faith after the 60
  Story 59
Veterans
  reception for 50
Clay County, North Carolina 22, 79, 86, 116
Cleveland 87
Clingman's Brigade 60
clock
  old 28
Clover, South Carolina 129
cobbler
  blackberry 133
Col.
  John Baxter 73
  Palmer 66
Coleman Columbus Galloway 106
Columbus
  George 54
Company E, 25th NC Infantry 50
Confederacy 57, 73, 74
Confederate
  Army 53, 54, 59, 62, 64
  deserter 47
  money 71
  soldiers 65
Continental Army 105
Cooke County Texas 36
Cooper's Gap, North Carolina 63
Corporals 61
Corporal T.W. Rhodes 61
cough syrup 84
creamed potatoes 89
Creek
  Big Indian 60
  Big Willow 64
  Flat 70, 71
  Paint 69
  Scott's 129
  Upper Bell 81, 116
Cumberland Gap 72
Cynthia Burgess 108

D

Dallas, Texas 28
Danny Owen 79

Dennis Smith 64
deserter 53, 55
deserters
  Civil War 56
Dial
  Mrs. 72, 73
dipped snuff 97
Don 29
Dora 137
Dovie Elizabeth Mathis Owen 108
Dow
  Lorenzo 54, 56
dowse 26
dowser
  water 97
dowsing 97, 100
Dukes mayonnaise 87
Dutch
  ancestry 52

E

Elijah Dillard Owen 122
Elizabeth
  Gilstrap Gravley 134
  Jane Owen 81, 110
  Lynch 106
  Owen 37
Ella
  Owen Medlock 119
  Polly Smith 137
Eller
  Lylish 116
Ellie 137
Elsie Medlock Alexander 119
Emma
  Cantrell 136
  Whitmire 106
English
  heritage 33
Esther Beasley 106

F

Falls
  Birdrock 138
  Olmsted 87
  Stillhouse 84, 85

family
  Bryson 53
  Owen 79
Federal Army 74
fever
  typhoid 126, 136
field hospital 59
fireboxes 39
Flat Creek 70, 71
Florence
  Caledonia Hall 124
  Galloway McKinney 52
Folk's battalion 66
Forest
  Nantahala 38
Fort Moultrie 60
Foster 88
Frances Price 106
Franklin 118
  North Carolina 26
  D. Roosevelt 138
Fredna
  Aunt 91
  Laura Owen Meredeith 37
Frenchman 132
French Broad River 113
Fritters
  Mr. 135

G

G. W. Whitmire 106
Gaelic 98
Gage
  Major 60
  Mary Siddall Hawkins 61
  Robert Samuel 60
Galloway 92
  Coleman Columbus 106
  James Fred 119
  Lyman Culwell 106
  Lyman Thayer 106
  Ruth Owen 119
Galloways 120
Gap
  Owen's 109
Gastonia, North Carolina 129

General Nathaniel Greene 105
George 29
  Orr 65, 66
  Washington 82
  Washington Whitmire 106
Georgia 81, 113, 114, 115
  families 35
  mountains of 114
  Northeast mountains of 37
  Towns County 37, 79, 80, 86, 90, 116
Georgia Mountains 79
German 130
Germans 136
Germany 132
ghost 108
ghostbuster 17
  in the mountains of Northeast Georgia 17
Ghosts 30, 108
Gilbert
  Henry, Rev. 60
Giles
  J.B. 91
Gill 27
Gillespie
  Jason 106
  John Harvey 106
  Katie 48
  Rebecca 106
Gladys
  Hoyle 128
  Marcella 136
Glazener
  Abraham 106
  Isaac 37
  Margaret Caroline Owen 35
  Prince Pulaski Edward 35
  Sallie 106
Gloucester
  Lumber Company 138
  Valley 57
  mountains of 84
Gordon Owen 26, 87, 100
government 32
Grandfather
  Mountain 33
  Owen 79, 86

Grandma
  Myra 59
Grandpa
  John 59
  Turpin
Grant
  Benjamin 50
  James 47
Gravley
  Elizabeth Gilstrap 134
  Perry Fields 134
  Richard 134
Grayson County, Texas 90, 116
Great-grandmother Sarah 86
Greene
  Nathaniel, General 105
Greenville
  South Carolina 135
  News 97
Greenwood County, South Carolina 89
grocery store
  mom and pop 30
Guilford Courthouse
  Battle of 105

H

hainted hollow 29
Hall
  Altha Owen 124
  Florence Caledonia 124
  Joshua 124
  Shawna 129
  William Elbert 124
harboring Yankees 58
Hawkins, Catherine Yancey 20
Haw River
  Battle of 105
Haywood County, North Carolina 31
heal 99
healing 97
Heather Hogsed 132
hen
  crows 30
Henderson 72
  Amanda Garner 54, 55
  Lafayette 54

Lafayette "Fate" 54
Nathaniel Howard 54, 55
Ray M. 54
Rene` 54
William Carson 54
Hendersonville 72
Henderson County 64
Hendricks
  Mrs. 97
Hendrix 55
Henry
  Patrick 105
Henserson
  Ruth 55
herbalist 97
heritage
  English 33
Hiawassee 91
Highway to Heaven 132
Hines Place 137
Hogback Mountain 35
Hogsed
  Heather 132
hollow
  Cherokee 33, 34
  hainted 29
Holly Springs 136
  School 134
Hoyle
  Gill 129
  Gladys 128
  Ollie 27, 129
  Ollie Smith 97
Hudgens
  William 30
Hufham, Robbie Gage 19
hunting
  possum 88
Hymn
  of Owen Family 142

I

Illinois
  Camp Douglas 48
Indian 53
Infantry

Company E, 25th NC 50
Irish 101, 131
Isaac Glazener 37
Island
  Johns 54
  Ship 62
  Sullivan's 60

J

J.B. Giles 91
Jackson
  Mary Lee 91

Jackson County, North Carolina 47, 108, 110, 125, 129
James
  F. Revis 74
  Fred Galloway 119
  Grant 47
  Milford 47
  Monroe 105
  Owen 22, 31, 37, 108, 111
  Roland Owen 110
  Wesley Middleton 74
  William Reid 35
Jane
  Grant Wilson 50
  Lynch 106
Jason Gillespie 106
Jasper
  William 35
Jehu McCall 37
Jeremiah McClellan Owen 115
Jernigan
  Tammy 99
Jerry Owen 17, 22, 28, 31, 35, 37, 61, 79, 86, 90, 110, 116, 130, 142
Jesse
  Luon Owen 90, 116
  Owen 80, 122
Johns Island, South Carolina 54
John
  B. Owen 57, 122
  Harrison Owen 122
  Harvey Gillespie 106
  Owen 17, 18, 57, 84

Sizemore 53
Turner 88
W. Owen 81, 112
Joshua Hall 124
Journey Home 97
Julia Owen 116
July Supper 92

K

Karen
  Medlock Pettit 119
  Patterson 105
Kathy
  Owen 106
  Owens 29, 97
Katie Gillespie 48
Kinston Middleton 64
Knoxville 65, 66, 70, 72, 73
  Tennessee 64
Kropelnicki
  Steve 35
  Winnie 35, 122
  Winnie Owen 57, 84

L

Lafayette Henderson 54
Lake
  Toxaway 34
land grant 105
Lay
  Charles 105
  Sarah Jane 106
Lee
  Mary 88
Legion
  Thomas' 59
Letter
  Camp Douglas 48
Limbock
  Richard 131
Linda
  Anders 50, 52
  Owen Anders 107, 123
Little Canada 129
little people 23
Little Ruf's Trick 107

Lizzie
  Owen 111
  Parker 35
Lorenzo
  Dow 54, 56
  Dow Henderson 56
Lorraine 101
Lou Ellen 128
Love County, Oklahoma 36
Lucretia Dillard Reid 35
Luke Osteen 65
Lylish Eller 116
Lyman
  Culwell Galloway 106
  Thayer Galloway 106
Lynch
  Ary Jane 106
  Bannister 106
  Elizabeth 106
  Jane 106
  Nathaniel, Sr. 106
  William 105, 106
Lynch's Law 105
Lynch-men 105

M

Macon County, North Carolina 31, 61, 117
Madison County 67
Major Gage 60
Malinda 58
  C. Chappel 48
Marauders 63
Marcella
  Gladys 136
Margaret M Owen 115
Marietta 36
Marsen 118
Marshall, North Carolina 60
Marson Owen 23
Martha Owen Queen 108
Maryville Road 72
Mary
  "Polly" Norris 31
  "Polly" Norris Rhodes 23
Mary Ellen Yelton 27, 97, 128, 129

Mary Lee 88
  Jackson 91
Mary
  McPherson 91, 99
  Siddall Hawkins Gage 61
Mathers
  Mrs. 67
Maude Ballard Owen 81
Maud Este Owen 119
McCall
  Jehu 37
McKinney
  Florence Galloway 52
McPherson
  Mary 91, 99
medicine
  mountain 99
Medlock
  Ella Owen 119
Melodie 26
Meredeith
  Fredna Laura Owen 37
Middleton 71
  James Wesley 74
  Kinston 64
  Mary 64
  Mr. 73
  Mrs. 67
  Narcissus "Beck" 64
Middle Fork Community 138
midwife 57
Milford
  James 47
militia
  North Carolina 31
milk sickness 125
Milton Rhodes 61
Mississippi
  Vicksburg 62
Mitch Aiken 138
Mobile, Alabama 62
mom and pop grocery store 30
money
  Confederate 71
Monroe
  James 105
Montana 135

Montgomery
  April 30, 63, 88, 91
moonshine 90, 92, 137
Morgan
  Beryl 110
Morristown 70, 73
Mountain
  Firebox 37
  Grandfather 33
  Hogback 35
  Paint 68
  Pinkbed 65
  Wolf 47, 108, 110, 111, 120
mountain
  doctor 57
  medicine 99
Mountains
  Civil War in the 45
  Georgia 79
  North Carolina 55, 56
mountains
  leaving the 116
mountains of
  North Carolina 100
Mountain Trace Nursing Center 110
Mr.
  Fritters 135
  Middleton 73
Mrs.
  Bailey 67
  Dial 72, 73
  Hendricks 97
  Mathers 67
  M.C. Chappel 48
  Middleton 67
  Robert Franklin (Mary Middleton)
    Orr 64
  Wright 87
Murphy, North Carolina 90
My Life's Record 40

N

Nantahala Forest 38
Narcissus "Beck" Middleton 64
Nathaniel
  Greene 105

Howard Henderson 54, 55
  Lynch, Sr. 106
Native American
  beliefs 23
Nelia 128
Nellie Dunn Sizemore 52
New Orleans 129
Norris
  Mary "Polly" 31
Northeast Georgia
  mountains of 79
North Carolina 70, 72, 74, 81, 114
  Andrews 129
  Balsam 27, 129
  Balsam Grove 87, 110
  Brevard 138
  Clay County 79, 86, 116
  Cooper's Gap 63
  families 35
  Franklin 26
  Gastonia 129
  Haywood County 31
  Jackson County 47, 108, 110
  Macon County 31, 61, 117
  Marshall 60
  militia 31
  Mountains 55, 56
  mountains of 100
  Murphy 90
  Rosman 137
  Scotts Creek 124
  Smithbridge 118
  Southwestern 57
  Southwest mountains of 37
  Transylvania County 35, 37, 50, 84,
    106, 115, 125
  Webster 110
Western
  farmers 30
Wolf Mountain 92

O

Ohio 87
ohn Harrison Owen 122
Oklahoma 35, 36
  Love County 36

Ol' Man 34
Old Hickory Division 136
Ollie
  Hoyle 27, 129
  Smith Hoyle 97
Olmsted Falls 87
omens 98
Oolenoy
  River 106, 134
  Valley 106
Orr
  George 65, 66
  Robert 64
  Robert F. 74
  Robert Franklin 64
  Robert Franklin (Mary Middleton), Mrs. 64
Osteen
  Luke 65
Ouija board 26
Owen 92
  Albert 115
  Alfred Henry 58, 122
  Alice 115
  Andrew Jackson 47, 92
  Arthur Tillman 107
  Aud Veste 119
  Danny 79
  Dovie Elizabeth Mathis 108
  Elijah Dillard 122
  Elizabeth 37
    Jane 110
  Gordon 26, 87, 100
  Grandfather 79, 86
  James 22, 31, 35, 37, 108, 111
  James Roland 110
  Jeremiah McClellan 115
  Jerry 28, 31, 35, 37, 61, 79, 86, 90, 110, 116, 130, 142
  Jesse 28, 80, 122
    Luon 22, 90, 116
  John 17, 18, 84
    B. 57, 122
    Harrison 122
    W. 112
  Julia 116
  Kathy 106
  Lizzie 111
  Malinda 57, 84
  Margaret M 115
  Marson 23, 24
  MaryAnn 47
  Maude Ballard 81
  Maud Este 119
  Paul 23, 24
  Pete 84, 123
  Pulaski Akin 37
  Richmond Pearson 108
  Rufus William 126
    William "Little Ruf" 107
  Sam 33, 86, 92
  Sarah 23, 24, 25
    Elizabeth Rhodes 22, 28, 90, 130
  School 111
  schoolhouse 111, 115
  Selly 23, 24
  Sherman 23, 24, 25
  Thomas Vannete 37
  Tillman 58
  William Jackson 28, 35, 80, 81, 110
  William Sherman 22, 79, 80, 86, 90, 115, 116
Owen's Gap 109
Owens
  Kathy 29, 97
  WJ 80
Owen country 84
Owen Family
  Hymn of 142
Owen Family Reunion 110

P

Paint
  Creek 69
  Mountain 68
Palmer
  Col. 66
paranormal 26, 98
Parker
  Lizzie 35
  William Solomon, Sr 37
Patrick Henry 105
Patterson

Karen 105
Selena 106
Paul 118
Pauline Dalice 137
Paul Owen 23
peach cobbler 92
Pennsylvania 87
Perry Fields Gravley 134
Petersburg 62
Pete Owen 84, 123
Pettit
  Karen Medlock 119
Phoebe Serena Bracken 50
Pickens
  South Carolina 97, 106
  County 120
Pickens County, South Carolina 134
pie
  possum 86
  sweet potato 28, 86
Pinkbed Mountain 65
Pittsylvania County
  Delegate 105
Pittsylvania County, Virginia 105
plantar wart 98
Poisoned Apples 27
polk sallet 89, 91
possum
  baked 28
  hunting 88
  pie 86
potatoes
  creamed 89
Powell
  Steve 134
prank 106
  Jim Wilson's 52
Price
  Ary Stewart 106
  Frances 106
  Thomas 106
Prince Pulaski Glazener 36
psychic 100
Pulaski Akin Owen 37

Q

Queen
  Martha Owen 108
Queens
  Amanda 108

R

Ralph
  Alexander 120
Ray M. Henderson 54
razor strap 23
Rebecca
  Gillespie 106
  Gillespie Whitmire 106
  Whitmire 106
redeye gravy 87
Red River 36
refugees 71
Reid
  James William 35
  Lucretia Dillard 35
Rene` Henderson 54
Reunion
  Owen Family 110
revenuers 79, 81
Reverend Bowen 109
Revis
  James F. 74
Revolutionary War 105
Rhodes
  Milton 31, 61
  Thomas Wilburn 61, 62
Rhodes Mary, "Polly" Norris 23
Richard
  Gravley 134
  Limbock 131
  Whiteside 63
Richmond
  Pearson Owen 108
  Virginia 54
Ripley
  Roswell 60
River
  Chucky 69
  French Broad 113
  Oolenoy 106, 134
River Hill Baptist Church 60, 61

Road
  Maryville 72
Robbie Gage Hufham 19
Robert
  Franklin Orr 64, 66, 74
  Samuel Gage 60
Rodt 130
Rosman, North Carolina 137
Rufus
  William "Little Ruf" Owen 107
  William Owen 126
Ruth Owen Galloway 119

S

sallet (salad)
  polk 89, 91
Sallie Glazener 106
Sam Owen 33, 86, 92
Saoirse 25, 59, 98
Sarah 90, 116
  Great-grandmother 86
  Elizabeth Rhodes Owen 22, 28, 90, 130
  Jane Lay 106
Saree Crack 130
school teacher 86
Scott's Creek 129
Scotts Creek
  Cemetery 124
  North Carolina 124
Selena Patterson 106
Selly 31, 118
  Owen 23
Shawna Hall 129
Ship Island 62
signs
  astrological 98
Sizemore
  Hattie 53
  John 52, 53
  Mary Jane 53
  Nellie Dunn 52
Smith
  Ella Polly 137
Smithbridge, North Carolina 118
smokehouse 22, 23

snapped beans 92
snuff
  dipped 97
social drink 84
soldiers
  Confederate 65
Southwestern North Carolina 57
Southwest North Carolina
  mountains of 79
South Carolina 60, 137
  Clover 129
  Greenville 135
  Greenwood County 89
  Johns Island 54
  Pendleton District 106
  Pickens 97, 106
  Pickens County 134
Spanish Fort 62
Springs
  Holly 136
Spring Bitters 84
stack cake 89
States
  War Between the 35, 50
Steve Kropelnicki 35
Steve Powell 134
Stillhouse Falls 84, 85
store
  grocery
    mom and pop 30
Styles
  Aaron 33, 34
Sullivan's Island 60
Supper
  July 92
sweet potato pie 28, 86
Sylva 110

T

Table Rock 97
Tammy
  Beavers 56
  Jernigan 99
tax
  whiskey 82
Tears

Trail of 31
telepathic 100
Tennessee 57, 74
  Knoxville 64
Texas 22, 56, 117, 119
  Bonham 81
  Cooke County 36
  Dallas 28
  Grayson County 90, 116
Thomas 31
Thomas' Legion 59
Thomas
  Price 106
  Vannete Owen 37
  Wilburn Rhodes 61
thrush 98
Thurston
  Uncle 26
Tillman Owen 58
Tina Webb 137
tonic 99
Towns County, Georgia 22, 37, 79, 80, 81, 83, 86, 90, 116
Toxaway
  Lake 34
trails
  Cherokee 83
Trail of Tears 31

Transylvania County, North Carolina 22, 33, 35, 37, 50, 64, 84, 106, 115, 125
  Cathey's Creek 54
trot-lined 91
Turner
  John 88
Turpin
  Grandpa 99
typhoid fever 126, 136

U

Union
  forces 62
  Army 47
Unionist 54
Upper Bell Creek 81, 116

V

Valley
  Gloucester 57, 84
  Oolenoy 106
Vernon 88
Vicksburg, Mississippi 62
Victrola 127
Virginia
  Pittsylvania County 105
  Richmond 54

W

Walker
  James Wylie 36
War
  Hendersons at 54
  Revolutionary 105
Ward
  Oner Owen 28
wart
  curing 99
  healing 98
  plantar 98
War Between the States 35, 50
Washington 26
  Cedro Wooly 26
  George 82
watermelon 88
water dowser 97
Webb
  Tina 137
Webster 110
Wedge
  Catherine Gage 19, 60, 100
Welsh 101
Western North Carolina 30
whiskey 79, 81, 84, 85
  tax 82
Whiteside
  Richard 63
Whitmire
  Emma 106
  G. W. 106
  George Washington 106
  Rebecca 106

Rebecca Gillespie 106
William 106
William "Fat Bill" 106
Wilburn 108
Will 73
William
  Jackson "Jackie" 28
  "Fat Bill" Whitmire 106
  Elbert Hall 124
  Hudgens 30
  Jackson Owen 28, 80, 81, 110
  Jasper 35
  Lynch 105, 106
  M. Henderson 54
  Sherman Owen 22, 79, 80, 86, 90, 115, 116
  Whitmire 106
Wilson
  Benjamin James "Jim" 50, 52
  Jane Grant 50
Winds of War 110
Winnie
  Kropelnicki 35, 122
  Owen Kropelnicki 57, 84
witch 27
WJ Owens 80
Wolf Mountain 47, 108, 110, 111, 120
  North Carolina 92
Wood
  Andrew Jackson "Andy" 129
Wright
  Mrs. 87
Wynne
  Catheryne Faison Hufhan 19
  William 21
  William Jr., 21

Y

Yankee
  bullet 61
  invaders 61
Yankeedom 70
Yankees 64, 73
  harboring 58
Yelton
  Mary Ellen 27, 97, 128, 129

Other Books Available from Andborough Publishing

ISBN : 0-9974181-0-3
58 pages paperback

Reiki is an ancient system of healing through the "laying on of hands" that is simple enough for children of all ages to learn. The Children's Reiki Handbook is a guide to energy healing that provides kids with the information they need to prepare for their first Reiki attunement; and shows them how to use their new skills to heal themselves and others.

This guide also includes: Healing with Reiki, Attunements; how to prepare for them and what to expect, Chakras and Auras…and more.

Only $12.⁹⁹

"I found Children's Reiki Handbook to be a concise yet thorough introduction to the Usui healing system of Reiki. It's perfect for children and young adults"
-ML Rhodes, Award Wining Author and Reiki Master

"If you want to learn Reiki, this book will serve as in inspiration towards that goal... This Reiki handbook is a great resource to introduce the benefits of Reiki healing to children or grown ups who are just starting out."
-Erin Kelly-Allshouse, *Children of the New Earth*

Let Us Praise Him in Poem is a wonderful collection of poems that serve as Bessie Lee's personal testimony of her belief in God and the path of Jesus Christ.

This is a collection of twenty poems that will inspire, comfort, cheer, and help you in your efforts to get closer to God. The poems are for all denominations.

ISBN : 0-9774181-1-1
58 page paperback $9.99

Order Additional Copies Today!
Only $17.95

Voices of Our Mountain Kin is a collection of legends, folk tales and memories of our heritage set in the Blue Ridge, Balsam and Great Smoky Mountains. You'll enjoy wonderful old-time stories of mountain medicines and healing, moonshining, ghosts, superstitions and faith, Civil War tragedies, pioneer living, love stories and much more

ISBN-13: 978-0-9774181-2-1
ISBN-10: 0-9774181-2-X
143 pages paperback

You can download an order form from our website or call toll free to order. We accept all major credit cards.

BOOK ORDER FORM

Children's Reiki Handbook   ___copies x $12.99 = $_____
Let Us Praise Him In Poem   ___copies x $9.99 = $_____
Voices of Our Mountain Kin   ___copies x $17.95 = $_____

                                              Total $_____

_____
Full Name (Please Print Clearly)

_____
Street Adress

_____
City   State   Zip

FOR CREDIT CARD ORDERS:

_____   ____/____ _____
Credit Card Number   Expiration Date Telephone

_____
Authorized Signature

To order call toll free (888) 348-7398; fax to (719) 219-5693; or mail to:
Andborough Publishing
4935 Sprangler Drive
Colorado Springs Colorado, 80922, USA
www.andborough.com

www.ingramcontent.com/pod-product-compliance
Lightning Source LLC
Chambersburg PA
CBHW031251290426
44109CB00012B/539